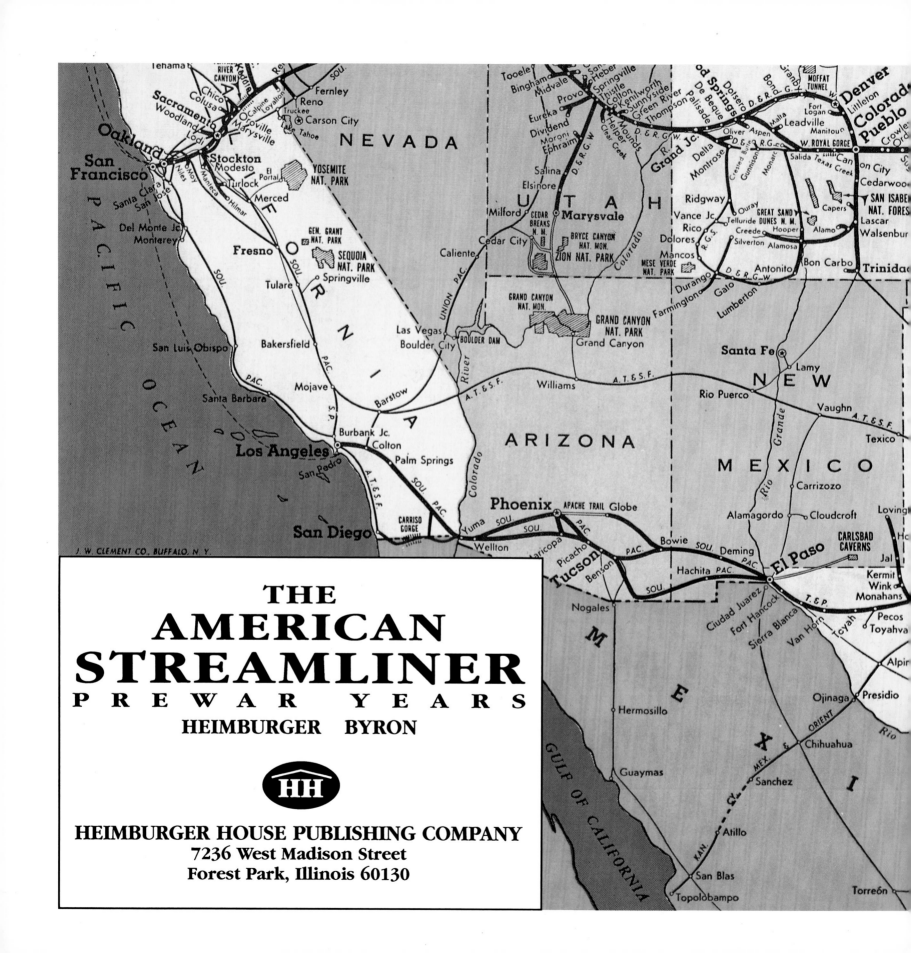

THE
AMERICAN
STREAMLINER
P R E W A R   Y E A R S
HEIMBURGER   BYRON

HH

HEIMBURGER HOUSE PUBLISHING COMPANY
7236 West Madison Street
Forest Park, Illinois 60130

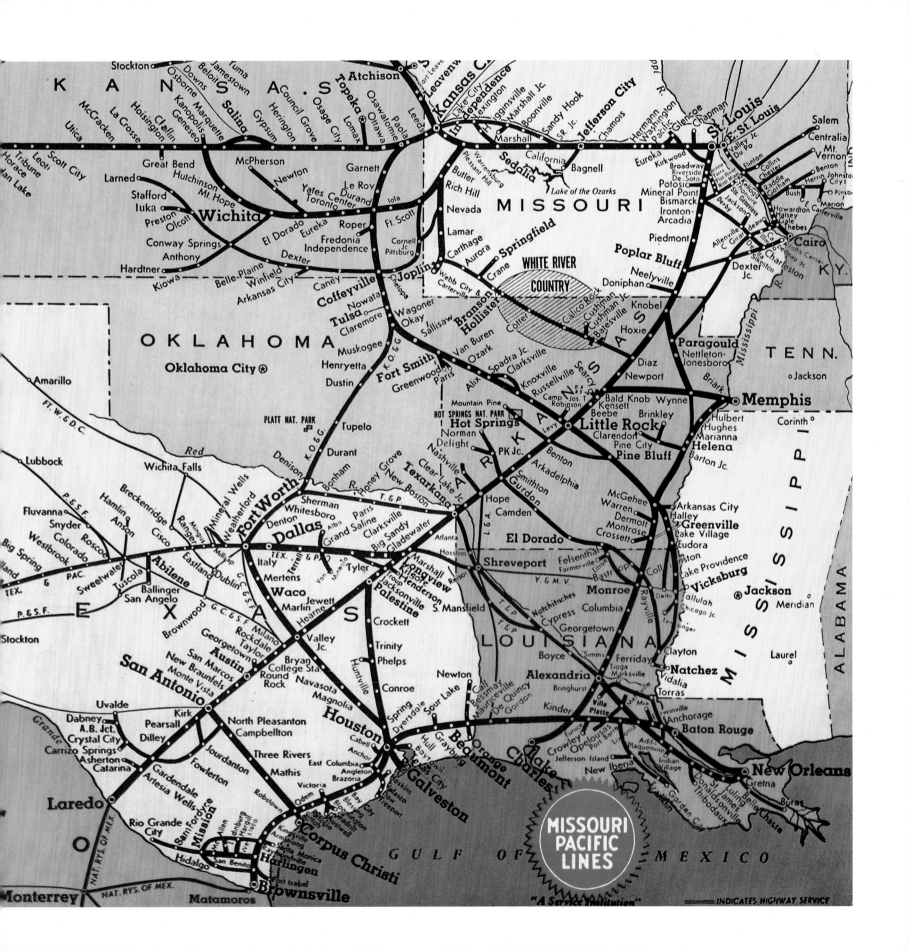

Dedication
To Bob
Getting there is half the fun.

Acknowledgements

I am grateful to a number of people who have contributed to this volume. As this book went through a number of stages, various people were instrumental in answering questions, loaning materials and giving advice. These included, among others, the Association of American Railroads, Dick Bowers, Chris Burritt, Budd Company, Jay Christopher, Donald Duke, EMD, Richard Ganger, Fred Hill, Kalmbach Publishing Co., Russ Larson, Tom Pearson, Russ Porter, Union Pacific Railroad and Robert Wayner. There were many others, as well, who were helpful, and I thank them all.

Book design: Charis Lehnert

Library of Congress Catalog Card Number: 96-94145
ISBN: 0-911581-39-1
First Edition
Printed in Hong Kong

HEIMBURGER HOUSE PUBLISHING COMPANY
7236 West Madison Street
Forest Park, Illinois 60130

Contents

Prologue: 1880-1932
Long Ago and Far Away...

Fancy, Fast and Flashy, North American streamlined passenger trains rolled off Depression era drawing boards and into both our hearts and our history.

Riding on the power of new and exciting technology, the streamliner reached its zenith during the decade immediately following World War II. Setting new records for speed, comfort and luxurious travel, the streamliner drew thousands down to the depot and back to trackside. From artifacts such as fading press releases and glossy photos, to miniature model trains speeding around millions of Christmas trees, their image and memory are etched deeply into the core of America's 20th Century. From rounded cab to boat-tailed observation, from dome diner to Slumbercoach, the Streamliner Era added a multitude of words and images to our collective heritage.

From beginnings predating the turn of the century, to today's budding reincarnation as an ultra-high speed "aircraft with wheels," streamliners speak volumes about the travel habits and technological accomplishments of several generations of Americans. The Streamliner Era ran from circa 1933 to 1960, when, to quote Cunard Line's advertising slogan for its great trans-Atlantic steamships, "Getting there was half the fun." It was an era in which those who know only winged cattle cars, or McBurgers, truly will have difficulty imagining.

Sit back in your comfortable Sleepy Hollow chair, as the matched, color-coordinated diesel

Jay Christopher   Previous page: Courtesy Fred Hill

locomotives slowly inch us into motion, and let's await the first call to dinner in the diner—"nothing could be finer."

An expertly-mixed cocktail awaits you in the Little Nugget lounge, or even under the stars in the Great Dome. Sleep comes amidst the snowy white sheets of your Pullman, as the porter shines your shoes, and the speedometer in the cab is pegged at 90 mph. Slower than the jet, and less

America's early railroads were powered by wood-burning locomotives then coal-fired steam engines such as this Chicago & NorthWestern 2900 class 4-6-2 E2 Pacific, pulling a passenger train at Ames, Iowa on April 31, 1948. The steam locomotive was the main means of railroad propulsion for many years, until the diesel finally encroached on its territory.

Chartered in 1867, the Pullman Palace Car Company owned the largest railroad car building facilities in the world.

convenient than the automobile, still the streamliner had a grand ambiance all its own.

To set our stage, the 19th Century Industrial Age was developed and propelled by falling water or its heated brethren, steam. Bigger was better, and industry hummed. America's railroads were powered by steam locomotives built by Alco, Baldwin or Lima, and their passengers rode in cars built by American Car & Foundry, Laconia, Pullman, Osgood Bradley, St. Louis Car and others.

However, by 1900 on virtually all the major railroads, passengers relaxed and slept in the sleeping cars owned, staffed and operated by just one manufacturer: Pullman. Pullman's near monopoly was so pervasive that even the new, small traveling case that ladies used to carry their essentials in was called a "Pullman."

While steam-hauled Pullman-built equipment monopolized land transportation a century ago, the forces of change were developing which ulti-

The "Daylight", Southern Pacific's new streamline train, which makes a daily dawn-to-dusk flight between San Francisco and Los Angeles.

20

mately dethroned both standard bearers and resulted in the lightweight diesel-electric streamliner.

A MEANS OF PROPULSION

The first component of future streamliners to be developed was the motive power. Although several roads, most notably the New York Central and the Southern Pacific, placed their streamliners behind steam, in general the new flagships introduced diesel-electric road passenger locomotives. Although commonly called "diesels" today, they actually required an amalgam of two technologies: internal combustion and electric power.

The concept of the internal combustion engine was first promoted by Nikolaus Otto in 1879, with his 4-stroke cycle design (intake, compression, ignition/power and exhaust). It is basically unchanged today under the hoods of hundreds of millions of gasoline powered cars and trucks

worldwide. However, experimenters such as Karl Benz—who ultimately named his new automobile after his niece, Mercedes—and even General Motor's engineering wizard—Charles F. "Boss" Kettering, soon learned that spark-ignited gasoline was not the fuel to challenge steam.

By the early 1890s a Munich, Germany, professor named Rudolph Diesel had successfully modified Otto's general concept into a workable "heat engine." Although still using the same basic cycle, Diesel's engine burned heavier petroleum fuel than gasoline.

His modification was a significant increase in the compression of air within the cylinder. Thus compressed by the moving piston, air temperature rose sharply, enough in fact, to be above the ignition point of the fuel being injected. Instant spark-free ignition was the result. This simplified ignition, and the heavier fuels were safer and contained more energy than gasoline.

The Southern Pacific's steam-powered Daylight *in an era when SP was said to bring grand hotel luxury to passenger train service. Its colorful orange, red and silver trains were not only beautiful but on time, as well.*

NEXT PAGE. Chicago & Eastern Illinois' Dixie Flagler *was a Chicago to Miami train operated every third day with all seats reserved in advance. The train featured reclining seat coaches, dining car, and an observation-buffet-lounge car. C&EI joined the streamlining era with this hooded steam locomotive that pulled fluted streamlined passenger cars.*

9

5304. McKeen Motor Car, made in Omaha, Neb.

The McKeen car, as it was called, was the brainchild of the Union Pacific's Chief Mechanical Officer William McKeen. It featured a distinctive nose that came to a point and large round windows for the passengers. Some roads that owned the McKeens were the Union Pacific (which was half owner in McKeen for a while), Southern Pacific, Texas & New Orleans, Chicago & NorthWestern, Milwaukee, Rock Island, Chicago Great Western and Bessemer & Lake Erie.

Diesel engines as first built were heavy and slow, but powerful machines. Indeed, as early as 1912 a German battleship was powered by a 12,000 hp "compression" engine of Diesel's design. It would take another 20 years before they were ready for the *Zephyr*.

Along with the development of diesel engines came that new wonder: electricity. Between the developmental work of men like Edison, Westinghouse, Tesla, Siemens and others, soon night was turned into day, and the sooty power of steam was being pushed aside by clean electric energy. Alternating current (AC) was preferred for industrial and residential use, since transformers could raise or lower voltages easily, but direct current (DC) was the choice for trolleys and railroad transportation needs. DC traction motors powered the Gay Nineties with ease, as our great grandparents rode about on an interconnecting web of trolleys and interurban lines. Soon those DC generators were directly connected to a diesel engine and combined the advantages of both budding technologies. The need for all that expensive overhead structure and wires, or 3rd rail, was gone.

IN THE EYE OF THE BEHOLDER, BEAUTY

And finally, the first inklings of airflow design and "streamlining" raised its head concurrent with the power revolution. Fredrick Adams patented a streamlined train design which was actually tested on the B&O in May and June of 1900. A photograph of Adams' train atop the famous Thomas Viaduct shows its wooden cars with fluted sides, nearly flush windows and a boat-tail observation car. A companion design arose five years later over 2,000 miles away.

Union Pacific's Chief Mechanical Officer William McKeen decided to develop a knife-prowed, distillate-powered, direct drive motor car for branch line use. Not only did the UP buy a number, but McKeen actually started an independent business and ultimately sold about 130 cars to such roads as the Rock Island and Chicago Great Western, among others. Sidetracked early by the failure of the chain and clutch drive, as well as the underpowered gas engine, still they contributed to the Streamliner Era.

A MONGREL ANCESTERY

As the Roaring 20s arrived, not only did Ford's Model T and its brethren take off, but improved

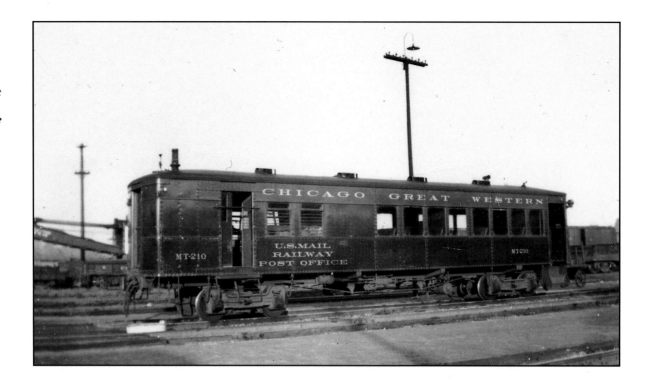

diesel and electrical equipment as well. A little company named Electro-Motive Engineering Co. started in Cleveland in 1922 with an idea to build gas-electric cars, sometimes called "doodlebugs." The following year a three-way consortium of American Locomotive, General Electric and Ingersoll-Rand produced the first diesel-electric switch- er. It looked like a box with wheels and con- tained a 300 hp inline 6-cylinder engine. Between it and others, however, a number of McKeen cars were pulled out of dead storage, re-engined with gas-electric power plants and a traction motor or two, and began paying their way once again—at least until the Great Depression.

PR-395

Budd

By the late 1920s enough progress had been made in the various disciplines that the first reasonable facsimile of a streamliner made its appearance. Built by the Chicago Great Western's Oelwein, Iowa shops in 1929, the *Blue Bird* was created from three castoff McKeen cars. The consist included a power/Railway Post Office (RPO)/express car containing a 300 hp Winton engine, a 74-seat coach and a parlor-club-observation car. The *Blue Bird* ran on the branch between Minneapolis and Rochester, Minnesota, home of the world-famous Mayo Clinic. The

observation car even included two Pullman sections reserved for clinic patients. It too lasted into the Depression.

A SHOT OF ELECTRICITY

While Mayo Clinic passengers were enjoying their internal combustion-powered ride, back in Philadelphia, the Edward G. Budd Company was applying for yet another patent. A formidable supplier to the auto industry, Budd had developed stamping and welding processes to manufacture the Unibody auto frame/body as we know it today. Always working with new materials,

A Philadelphia automotive parts manufacturer, Edward G. Budd, entered the passenger car market with his first full-sized car delivered to the Santa Fe in early 1936. Numbered #3070, it could carry 52 passengers. It was built at this plant.

13

In 1933 Colonel Earl J.W. Ragsdale, Budd's chief engineer, and his staff, perfected Shotwelding. Here the Boston & Maine's and Maine Central's stainless steel Flying Yankee, built at a cost of $275,000, survives into the 1990s. The 200-foot-long train, with a 600-horsepower diesel engine, was touted as being able to accelerate to speeds of 110 miles per hour.

Budd's chief engineer of research, Col. Earl J.W. Ragsdale had been experimenting with stainless steel for the past year or so.

Stainless steel is a combination of iron, chromium and nickel, which is virtually rustproof and much stronger than ordinary mild steel. In 1930, its major drawback—aside from cost—was that it could not be welded by any process then known. Col. Ragsdale, however, developed a process whereby a high amperage electric current was applied for an extremely brief time. This "shot" of electricity melted and fused the stainless steel sheets nearly instantaneously, and contained the fused portion under the electrodes. This newly-patented process was named Shotwelding, in direct reference to its electrical nature. The streamliner's components were now all gathered

At the rear of the Flying Yankee, *the solarium lounge offered passengers broad vision windows, with accompanying window draperies and comfortable parlor chairs. The windows were made of safety glass, sealed to keep out the cold and condensation.*

Don Heimburger

in the wings, as the Crash of '29 ended the decade and heralded the Great Depression.

A SEASON OF TRIBULATION
THEN HOPE

As the Depression gathered intensity during 1930 and 1931, industrial production plummeted. General Motors purchased both Electro-Motive Corporation and the Winton Engine Company in 1930, based upon their perceived value in respective market share and patents owned.

The following year, the development of simplified air conditioning units finally made their application to railroad passenger cars cost effective, and Pullman began adding this improvement to most of its cars as they were renovated. Likewise, in a concentrated effort to develop new business, Budd Shotwelded together an experimental air-

In 1932, Budd built the two-car Silver Slipper *for the Texas & Pacific. The second car ran on Michelin rubber tires. The train was driven by two American LaFrance 240 hp GE engines.*

plane, bus and rail car of stainless steel. Only the rail car showed potential. Little noticed, but of utmost importance, the United States Congress appropriated half a million dollars for the Navy to assist in diesel engine development in its submarine program.

The depths of Depression hopelessness arrived with the "Hoovervilles" of 1932. The only bright spot on the railroad passenger horizon was from a couple of stainless steel self-propelled gas cars Budd built for the Reading Railroad and the Pennsylvania. The carbodies were great, but the rubber-tired wheels and gasoline-mechanical drives were patently impractical. The other item of potential promise was that Navy contract to develop a high speed diesel engine of sufficient size to power a submarine. Several builders besides GM/Winton were also interested, including Fairbanks-Morse and American Locomotive (Alco). For all concerned, it was a frustratingly slow effort.

Still a decade in the future at that time, Winston Churchill's comment regarding Britain's first WWII victory during mid-1942 in North Africa, sums up the period aptly: "It is not the end, nor even the beginning of the end. However, perhaps it is the end of the beginning!"

41-7747

EMD

Chapter One: 1933-1935

'She sure is coming...
wasn't she !'

The spring of 1933 found "That Man" (FDR) in the White House, his New Deal legislation before Congress and a self-promoting Century of Progress Exposition about to open on Chicago's lakefront. A new, self-induced optimism was slowly washing across the country from Washington D.C. to Washington State. Things were going to get better.

FROM POTS AND PANS TO PULLMAN PANACHE

In early 1933, nearly alone in the erecting halls of Pullman-Standard, stood two radically new and experimental cars. The more famous was the *George M. Pullman,* a sleeper-lounge-observation which weighed but 48 tons, little more than half a conventional car. A similar car, the *City of*

Cheyenne was an observation-coach which weighed even less at 37 tons. Constructed of riveted aluminum, these cars marked Pullman's entry into the lightweight car era, and are widely considered to be the first lightweight passenger cars built of full height, width and length.

The *George M. Pullman* contained an enclosed observation lounge, all-room accommodations and a small buffet area. The *City of Cheyenne* carried 50 coach seats and a small rear solarium. Both all-aluminum cars were specifically built to display the latest Pullman technology to visitors at the Century of Progress Exposition. Their exteriors were burnished aluminum, while polished aluminum accented the interiors.

After the close of the fair in 1934, the sleeper-

The George M. Pullman, *the first all-aluminum sleeping car in America.*

PREVIOUS PAGE. The steam locomotive's days were numbered with the influx of the streamliners, seen lined up for an EMD publicity photo.

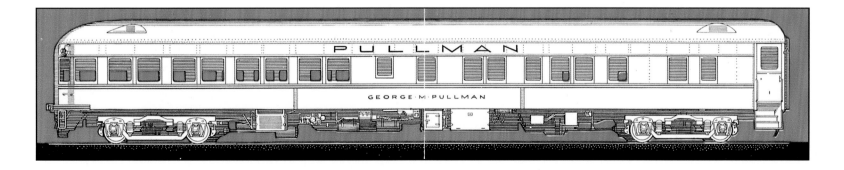

Built of ALCOA *Aluminum*
this New Pullman "Travels Light" and Safely

Builders of riding comfort and safety for three-quarters of a century, Pullman takes another step forward with the new "George M. Pullman"—made almost entirely of the light, strong alloys of Alcoa Aluminum. Cutting 50% from the weight of the standard Pullman, Alcoa Aluminum makes for swifter, smoother riding with even greater safety, greater durability of structural parts. Alcoa Aluminum comes in every form needed for car construction—extruded shapes and sections, rolled plates, structural shapes in any desired length up to 90 feet. For these reasons, too, *all* transportation units—buses, trucks, tank cars, mine cars, elevators—every form of mass in motion is rapidly being redesigned from the wheels up in Alcoa Aluminum.

The "George M. Pullman"—one of two all-aluminum Pullmans exhibited at A Century of Progress Exposition. Weight 96,980 lbs., including air-conditioning equipment. With ordinary materials it would weigh 180,000 lbs. Due to its light weight, it needs only 4-wheel trucks. (These are fabricated of Aluminum.) Yet it surpasses American Railway Association standards for strength and safety. Smart, modern decorative scheme in aluminum. Even the insulation is crumpled aluminum foil.

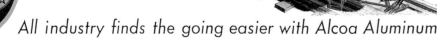

All industry finds the going easier with Alcoa Aluminum

Bringing efficiency and economy to industry, saleability to industry's products, Alcoa Aluminum is finding its way into most progressive plants. Light in weight, yet strong as structural steel, non-contaminating, non-magnetic, a good conductor of heat and electricity, this is the ideal metal for production equipment. To the finished product, Alcoa Aluminum brings ease of handling, durability, attractiveness. In the plant itself Alcoa Albron as a paint pigment protects against rust, weathering, smoke and acid fumes—makes brighter working conditions.

There's a place in *your* plant and *your* product for Alcoa Aluminum. Let us show you how to use, form and handle this metal. Address: ALUMINUM COMPANY *of* AMERICA; 1802 Gulf Building, PITTSBURGH, PENNSYLVANIA.

MODERN VENTILATION USES THE MODERN METAL

Alcoa Aluminum makes this air-filter lighter, easier to install. This metal resists corrosion, isn't affected by moisture in the air, absorbs sound from vibration, not to mention its attractiveness, appearance and long life.

SOMETHING NEW IN LIGHTING FIXTURES

Here Alcoa Aluminum helps with its light weight, its light-reflecting surface. A color-filter gives this fixture the appearance of expensive translucent glass but the light is really indirect. Made of deep-etched aluminum, it is equally attractive day and night.

FOR EYE-HAZARDOUS JOBS

These goggle frames, made of Alcoa Aluminum, are light in weight, easy to wear through the day's work—yet strong. Alumilite finish gives them attractiveness, longer life and corrosion resistance—an important detail in many plants.

ALCOA
ALUMINUM

observation was assigned to the Pullman pool. Later service found the car tailing the Union Pacific *Treasure Island*, the Santa Fe *Chief* and the *Florida Arrow*, among others.

Pullman placed the coach-observation in service on the Illinois Central and the Union Pacific. For some length of time, the *City of Cheyenne* was the tail car on UP's *City* connecting service

between Cheyenne and Denver. Thanks to this car, the otherwise unremarked service became unofficially known as the *City of Cheyenne*.

Both cars earned reputations for rough riding as compared to 85-ton Pullman sleeping or parlor cars. Still the twin lightweights marked a milestone in passenger car development and lasted well into the Streamliner Era.

"Tomorrow's Train...Today!" was the Union Pacific's cry to the world when it launched the new M-10000, North America's first streamliner. The train was painted in Amour yellow, as a safety measure.

Travel comfort was given a new significance when the Union Pacific introduced new high speed, lightweight, fully air-conditioned trains such as this. Other features included meals served from a special tea-cart steam table, indirect lighting and seating for 116 passengers in comfort and beauty. The Union Pacific prided itself in serving more of the scenic West and its national parks than any other railroad including Zion-Bryce, Grand Canyon, Yellowstone, Grand Teton, Rocky Mountain National Park and Boulder Dam.

ONE YELLOW CATERPILLER, PLEASE

Trying to minimize losses on poorly patronized, but mandated branch line services, numerous railroads including the Union Pacific and the Burlington, were desperate to develop a replacement for the tired and costly steam-powered locals. The gas-electric car had promise, but the fuel was too expensive, the ride was rough and slow and the pizazz of the automobile was nonexistent. For the brave, an opportunity beckoned.

Thus, early in 1933 the Union Pacific signed a contract with Pullman-Standard for North America's first streamliner. UP was no stranger to streamlining thanks to the McKeen cars of 1905, which they had kept running for more than a decade. Then, in the '20s most McKeen cars were replaced by new Electro-Motive-powered gas cars. The small compact streamliner was a logical progression in this process.

Riveted together in the best Pullman tradition, the lightweight aluminum speedster stretched 204 feet and weighed but 85 tons, equal to a single standard Pullman car. Power for the articulated 3-car train was provided by a GM/Winton V-12 distillate (gas) engine of 600 hp.

The M-10000 rode on four, two-axle trucks with the lead set containing two traction motors. Standing only slightly over 12' tall, the unit was significantly smaller in both height and cross section than traditional equipment. Its design was reviewed by aircraft engineers and tested in the wind tunnel at the University of Michigan.

After delivery to the UP on February 25, 1934, *Motor 10000* embarked on a 68-city cross coun-

SPEED with comfort, safety and economy of operating costs were the aims in the construction of Union Pacific's new train. Because of its radical departure from the conventional type of car and train construction, exhaustive tests were conducted during the development of every feature of the train to insure its perfection. Slightly more than 204 feet in length, from rounded nose to its fin-like tail, the total weight of the three-car unit is equal only to that of a single modern steel Pullman car. ● The light weight was obtained by the use of aluminum alloy which has one-third the weight of steel, with the same strength. The tubular structural design was perfected to give additional strength. ● The smooth, stream-lined exterior of the train, with even the vestibule steps drawn up into the cars while the train is in motion, provides sufficient power economy to enable a 600 horse power distillate-burning motor, directly connected to a generator, to provide power to propel the train at a maximum speed of 110 miles per hour. ● The super-brakes are of a new design—a dual system, each coordinated part of which is capable of safe operation in event of failure of the other. A duplicate device is installed to require the engineer to keep both foot and hand constantly on a control. Releasing pressure of hand or foot automatically closes the throttle and applies the brakes. A newly developed appliance called a "decelerometer" has been perfected and is installed on the train.

Its function is to equalize brake pressure on every wheel, admit maximum pressure but prevent locked wheels. The braking system is such that the train cannot be started unless the brakes are in perfect working condition. ● Articulation between the cars of the train was adopted as best suited for smooth riding at high speeds. In articulation, the cars are hinged together with only one truck between each two cars. ● The train is fully equipped with roller bearings and trucks are designed to incorporate the use of rubber to the fullest extent for the elimination of noise and to improve riding quality. The train is operated from a cab situated above and in front of the engine compartment. An instrument board before the engineer shows conditions of every part of his power plant at all times. There are air, oil, water, fuel, electric gauges and a speedometer. He has an unobstructed view ahead and on both sides of him. Electric signals afford communication between him and the train crew. ● A powerful fog-piercing headlight is supplemented by a light which throws a ten-inch vertical beam, for added safety. Warning signals are given by a powerful siren and an electric gong. The diagram below shows the plan of the new 3-car train, the location of its various features from engine room, mail and baggage compartments of the first car to buffet kitchen in the end car. ● The new train is Union Pacific's answer to the desire of today for greater speed, with safety, and comfort.

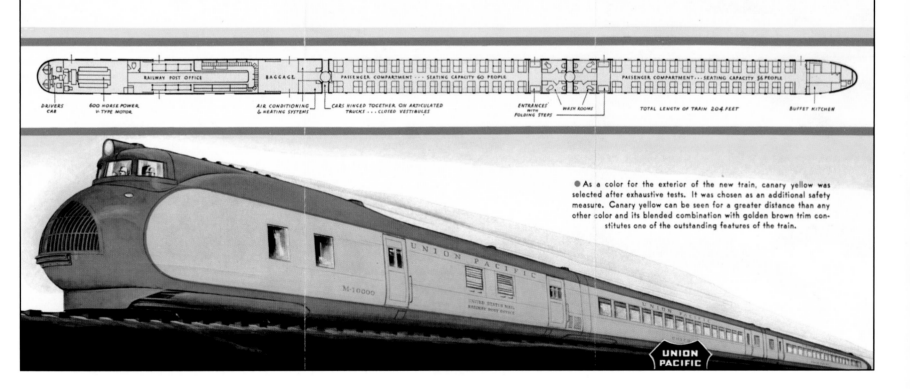

● As a color for the exterior of the new train, canary yellow was selected after exhaustive tests. It was chosen as an additional safety measure. Canary yellow can be seen for a greater distance than any other color and its blended combination with golden brown trim constitutes one of the outstanding features of the train.

try tour which introduced America to UP's bright new Armour Yellow paint scheme. Containing a baggage area in the power car, seats for 116 and a kitchenette, it was simplicity personified. Interestingly enough, the kitchenette was located in the boat-tail rear of the train, a design error soon rectified. Interior colors were soft pastels, accented with polished aluminum and the lighting was indirect and predominantly fluorescent.

The M-10000 hit 111 mph in tests, was front page news everywhere it visited, and drew crowds totalling nearly 2 million. When the M-10000 entered revenue service between Kansas City and Salina, Kansas on January 31, 1935, it was formally named the *City of Salina*.

Patronage immediately overwhelmed the train, and UP gladly dusted off the "sold out" sign. UP/Pullman/EMC already had the next new and improved model in the works. Indeed, the UP had been so confident that it contracted for the M-10001 in June, 1933, only months after the initial M-10000 order had been placed.

Due to its limited seating, non-diesel power and the inflexible nature of an articulated consist, the M-10000 had only a nine year lifespan. Decommissioned and scrapped in 1942, its aluminum was of more value to the war effort than in passenger service. Still, a fleet of Armour Yellow and Harbor Mist Grey—originally brown— *City* streamliners flashing across the UP system were all sired by the success of M-10000. Many would be built by Pullman and most powered by Electro-Motive. An era began with the M-10000 which still continues in limited form today, some 60 years later.

GOD OF THE WEST WIND, ZEPHRUS

As one of the largest Midwestern roads, the Chicago, Burlington & Quincy knew all too well the toll that the combined Depression and automobile had exacted on its passenger business. With ticket sales off nearly 50% between 1929 and 1933, it joined UP in taking a close look at the advantages of internal combustion and streamlining.

Knowing that a railroad passenger car required exterior maintenance during its life equal in cost to its original construction, Burlington President Ralph Budd* traveled to Philadelphia in late 1932 to view the stainless steel gas cars being built by the Budd Company. Impressed by what he saw, on June 17, 1933 the CB&Q placed an order with Budd for a 3-car articulated stainless steel streamliner with motive power supplied by GM/Winton.

The all-stainless steel train as finalized was 197 feet long, averaged 11 feet, 6 inches high and was articulated. The power car contained both an RPO and storage mail section, while the center car combined a large baggage/express compartment, a small buffet section and 20 coach seats. The observation lounge area seated 12, while the remainder of the car carried 40. Total passenger seating was 72.

The Zephyr:
- *Built of stainless steel*
- *Rides on articulated trucks*
- *Runs on roller bearings*
- *Air-conditioned in all compartments*
- *Equipped for radio reception*
- *Electro-pneumatic brakes*

* No relation to Edward G. Budd.

Tom Pearson

Although Winton could have easily provided a distillate engine similar to that in the UP's *City of Salina*, Budd realized that additional benefits could be obtained by the use of diesel power. After two years of effort, GM's Kettering and his staff had managed to create a 600 hp inline 8-cylinder engine as a direct offshoot of that 1931 Navy developmental contract. GM had two experimental models powering the Chevrolet exhibit at the Chicago Century of Progress Exposition. Budd apparently arranged to meet Kettering and EMC Chief Engineer Dilworth in front of those hammering display engines.

Based upon Kettering's brilliant engineering reputation and Dilworth's salty comment "she ain't much now, but she has hopes," Budd announced the Burlington's commitment to diesel power for the *Pioneer Zephyr*. Kettering and Dilworth accepted Budd's order with a sense of urgency. In later years, Kettering would remember the diesel project with a telling comment, "Let it suffice to say that I do not remember any trouble with the dip stick." He likewise described Ralph Budd as "a very nervy railroad president." Both comments were accurate.

While the diesel took shape in Cleveland, wind tunnel tests at MIT in Cambridge, Massachusetts determined the proper aerodynamic shape for Budd's stainless steel gamble. Soon Budd began Shotwelding sheets of stainless steel as architectural firms Holabird & Root plus Paul Cret began the *Zephyr's* interior design. Indirect fluorescent lighting in ceiling coves with coordinated pastel colors of warm grey and green on the walls, ceiling, carpeting and seats were designed and approved.

Air conditioning vents were concealed behind stainless steel grills, and tubular aluminum seat frames were ordered. The twin-paned safety glass was shielded by color-coordinated silk curtains, and the seat backs were notched to hold tray tables. Even a radio was provided. No such design effort had ever before been made to give railroad coach passengers such a pleasing travel experience.

Finally, on April 7, 1934 the *Zephyr* was completed and rolled out for its first test run. Reportedly it had taken an inauspicious four days to get the Winton engine to fire, but once started,

Interior views of the luxurious Burlington Zephyr, *named as the* Wings of the Iron Horse *by the railroad. The train weighed about 95 tons, or about as much as one typical heavyweight Pullman. Holabird & Root and Philadelphia's Paul Cret were consulting architects for the Burlington in the train's styling.*

Tom Pearson

In 1934, Reincke-Ellis-Younggreen & Finn Advertising in Chicago was asked by the Burlington Railroad to plan a public relations blitz for the new Zephyr passenger train. The advertising firm suggested that the Zephyr project be looked at "not just as an exhibition of a single revolutionary type train, but as an unparalleled opportunity to register Burlington LEADERSHIP and to present successive crowds in these centers of population the big goodwill building story of the Burlington System.

The goodwill tour included the following cities:

Christened the Burlington Zephyr *by Marguerite Cotsworth of Oak Park, Illinois, a Swarthmore College student, on April 18, 1934, the train went on a five-week barnstorming tour of Eastern cities. Marguerite was the daughter of Passenger Traffic Manager Albert Cotsworth Jr.*

Chris Burritt

Worcester	Boston & Albany Passenger Station	8:30 AM - 1:00 PM	Cleveland	Cleveland Union Terminal	8:30 AM - 9:00 PM
Springfield	Boston & Albany Passenger Station	3:30 AM - 8:00 PM	Pittsburgh	Pennsylvania Station	8:30 AM - 8:00 PM
Albany	New York Central Passenger Station	8:30 AM - 2:00 PM	Columbus	Union Station	8:30 AM - 2:00 PM
Schenectady			Dayton	Union Station	5:00 PM - 9:30 PM
Utica	New York Central Passenger Station	5:30 PM - 9:30 PM	Cincinnati	Union Station	8:30 AM - 8:00 PM
Syracuse	New York Central Passenger Station	8:00 AM - 1:00 PM	Louisville	Union Station, 10th & Broadway	8:30 AM - 8:00 PM
Rochester	New York Central Passenger Station	4:00 PM - 9:45 PM	Indianapolis	Union Station	8:30 AM - 9:00 PM
Buffalo	Lindbergh Drive Central Terminal	8:30 AM - 9:00 PM	Fort Wayne	Pennsylvania Station	8:30 AM - 1:30 PM
Detroit	Michigan Central Terminal	8:30 AM - 9:00 PM			
Toledo	New York Central Passenger Station	8:30 AM - 7:00 PM			

#9900 never looked back. On April 9, 1934 the *Zephyr* warmed its roller bearing journals on the Reading between Perkiomen Junction and Philadephia by reaching a speed of 104 mph. Nine days later on April 18, 1934 it was turned over to the Burlington in a ceremony at Pennsylvania's Broad Street Station in Philadelphia. Duly christened *Zephyr* with the swing of a champagne bottle, the "God of the West Wind" began writing its own page in our history books.

The Burlington promptly whisked the *Zephyr* onto a five week Eastern tour, culminating in an 80 mph average dash down the 140 mile speedway known as the Pennsy's Fort Wayne Division. To mark the opening of the second year of the Chicago Century of Progress Exposition, on May 26, 1934 the *Zephyr* left Denver Union Station and roared east. When the dust settled at Chicago 13 hours and 5 minutes later, a distance of 1,015 miles had been covered nonstop in 785 minutes.

In 1934 the Century of Progress Exposition was held in Chicago at which Burlington's Zephyr was exhibited; the lines were long to see the sleek new air-conditioned train that was radio-equipped and ran on roller bearings.

The "9900" Pioneer Zephyr *went on display at A Century of Progress Exposition in Chicago then made a coast-to-coast tour.*

The following four photographs were taken showing *the* Burlington Zephyr *while under construction by the Edward G. Budd Manufacturing Company in Philadelphia. The lead unit, shown here outside the plant, needs a few more finishing touches. The* Zephyr *rolled out for its first test run on April 7, 1934.*

29

Budd

*Interior of the lead Zephyr
unit looking toward the front
reveals two large overhead
fans used for cooling.*

Budd

The Zephyr lead unit skeleton shows how the train was supported. The middle set of square openings will be used for cab windows. Note the unit is still up on blocks in the factory.

31

Budd

A few finishing touches are still required as the end Zephyr *car sits on a siding at the Budd plant. The train was a combination of the best that art and science had to offer at the time.*

A peak of 112 mph was reached, while the average speed of 77.6 mph set a world record, and brought an estimated half a million Midwesterners to trackside. It also added a new comment to our lexicon..."She sure is coming.....wasn't she!"

After spending the summer at the Exposition alongside the UP M-10000, the *Zephyr* became a movie star. Rechristened as the *Silver Streak* by Hollywood, the film had all the latest technology of 1934: the Boulder Dam, an iron lung, a prophetic German spy and beautiful girl. Except for the fate of the spy, *Trains* magazine columnist Wallace Abbey summed it up best, "All characters, including the train, lived happily ever after."

Finally, on November 11, 1934 the *Silver Slipper* entered the assignment for which it was built, local service between Lincoln, Nebraska and Kansas City, Missouri, via Omaha and St. Joseph. It averaged 97% availability, covered 77,600 miles, cut operating costs by 40% and boosted passenger counts by more than 50% over the next 12 months. The Streamliner Era was off in grand style.

Passenger volume was such that early in 1936

The Zephyr's average speed of 77.6 miles per hour set a world record in 1934 to coincide with its title of God of the West Wind.

33

LIKE GIVING *Wings* TO YOUR FAVORITE EASY CHAIR *at* HOME

The Boston and Maine Railroad and the Maine Central Railroad present for your comfort and enjoyment the new "Flying Yankee," first streamlined, Diesel-powered train of any railroad in the East.

Built by the joint effort of the General Motors Corporation, through its Winton Engine Division, and by the E. G. Budd Manufacturing Company, the train embodies all that is new in modern passenger transportation and, in addition, has many new features for passenger comfort and speed, with safety. This leaflet is intended as a souvenir of your visit to the new train and to acquaint you with a few of the salient facts regarding it.

The new "Flying Yankee" is built of stainless steel. It cost $275,000. Its various parts are joined together by the "Shotweld" process, by which there is produced a structure of maximum strength and durability, with a minimum of weight. The train is 200 feet in length and weighs 212,000 pounds. (The average Pullman car alone weighs 152,000 pounds.)

The power plant is a 600 horsepower Diesel engine, which burns fuel oil. The Diesel engine, in turn, transmits its power to electrical units which perform the work of actually turning the wheels. The train is capable of speeds as high as 110 miles per hour, although in actual operation its average speed will be from 60 to 90 miles an hour.

In the forward section is located the power plant, with windows giving the operator a view in all directions. Directly behind the power plant is the baggage section and then the buffet, from which meals will be served at the seats in the train. Then, in order, come the forward passenger sections of the articulated unit, the center passenger sections and in the rear, a solarium lounge. The train has seating accommodations for 144 passengers and all seats in the train are reserved and sold by number. Smoking will be permitted in the forward passenger section and in the solarium lounge.

All the windows are of a new, broad-vision type, sound-proof with special shatterproof safety glass, hermetically sealed so that neither condensation nor frost will form and blur them.

The seats in the coach sections are of the lounging de luxe type, upholstered with fine, heavy mohair and are so designed that passengers may ride in comfort never before provided in "day coach" accommodations. The solarium observation section in the rear is equipped with comfortable parlor chairs. Windows are curtained and have artistic draperies in addition.

The air conditioning apparatus in the train is of a new and improved type which completely cleans and changes the air every two minutes. It keeps the air at an even temperature, so that it is always cool in the summer and warm in the colder months. Rubber insulation is used throughout the train in a manner so that noise is reduced to a minimum.

Meals on the train will be served at the seats, each being equipped to take a portable, individual luncheon tray. For parties of three or four the train is equipped with tables which are snapped into position between reversible seats. Hand luggage will be cared for by the uniformed train porters, who will be on the train and store luggage in special compartments provided for it. Overhead racks for hats and parcels are provided, as are individual "robe racks" for coats in front of each passenger seat in the "coach" sections of the unit.

All lighting on the train is of the indirect type. Bulbs are concealed within longitudinal coves below the ceiling and along the sides, and are so designed that they produce a maximum of illumination at reading height.

Its schedule (now only tentative) will be to leave Portland at 8:30 a.m.; Biddeford at 8:47 a.m.; Dover, N.H. 9:19 a.m., with arrival in Boston at 10:20 a.m. The new train will leave Boston at noon for a non-stop run to Portland, arriving at 1:45 p.m.; and then continuing on at 1:50 p.m. to Lewiston, with arrival at 2:35 p.m.; a flag stop at Winthrop at 3 p.m.; Waterville 3:35 p.m.; with arrival in Bangor at 4:45 p.m.

The tentative schedule calls for departure from Bangor at 5 p.m.; Waterville 6:25 p.m.; a flag stop at Winthrop at 7 p.m.; Lewiston at 7:25 p.m.; arrival in Portland at 8:10 p.m.; departure from Portland at 8:15 p.m.; Dover, N.H. at 9:02 p.m., with arrival in Boston at 10:05 p.m. The final trip of each day will be departure from Boston at 11 p.m., with arrival at Dover, N.H. at 12:03 a.m. and in Portland at 12:50 a.m.

We believe passengers will find in the new "Flying Yankee" the ideal way to travel.

Tom Pearson

---

an all-coach fourth car was added to this original *Zephyr*. Boosting seating to 132, it made the little streamliner perhaps the most profitable train on the Burlington. Certainly, it was the most talked about.

After a 26 year, 3.2 million mile career, the *Silver Streak* was ceremoniously retired to the Chicago Museum of Science and Industry on May 26, 1960 and placed next to a diesel/electric-powered submarine. Even more indicative of her place in railroad history was the June 20, 1964 donation of an 8-cylinder GM/Winton diesel engine to the Smithsonian Institution in Washington D.C.

BY ZEPHYR, WAY DOWN EAST

Impressed by the Burlington *Zephyr's* passenger appeal and cost savings, the jointly operated Boston & Maine/Maine Central railroads decided to invest in a copy. Once Roosevelt's Reconstruction Finance Corporation approved the railroad's financing request, the B&M placed its Budd/Winton order in August, 1934. Reflecting the passenger concentration on the railroad's premier Boston-Portland-Bangor route, the *Flying Yankee* contained 138 seats, but no RPO section.

Arriving in February, 1935 the *Flying Yankee* was exhibited across the joint B&M/MeC system. A special full color brochure was distributed on the April 4, 1935 inaugural run, extolling its various new and exciting features.

Very popular with patrons was the full buffet, with at-your-seat tray service. Passengers gazed in awe at the blue-green painted walls contrasting with ivory colored ceilings. Brown leather arm rests were separated by seats upholstered in mulberry taupe mohair. The drapes were colored lemon gold with triple green stripes. Green and sand colored carpeting covered the floor, and all was illuminated by indirect lighting recessed in a continuous cove. The lounge-observation set a contrast by having a darker blue-green above the window line, a henna-rust carpet, and triple brown stripes in the lemon gold window drapes. Individual chairs were upholstered in green.

As an added benefit, "The services of train porters....will be available...throughout (your) journey...to do the small errands, to aid mothers with children, and to make everyone's journey one of complete relaxation and pleasure."

From that first run, the *Yankee* was a sellout. Reducing travel time from Boston to Bangor by 65 minutes to a total of 4 hours and 25 minutes, with all this new luxury at no extra cost, galvanized frugal Yankees. In 12 months the train carried over 94,500 passengers and grossed $266,800. Traffic surged 48%, and a steam-powered second section had to be frequently run. With a per mile revenue rate of $1.42 vs expenses of $.36, even the bankers were happy. In its first 24 months of operation, she covered 431,000 miles on her daily 730-mile ping-pong route between Boston and Bangor.

The *Yankee's* saga continued unabated until WWII. Then her limited seating pushed her off the Portland corridor and into other work. Routes included the Boston-Littleton, New Hampshire *Mountaineer* via Crawford Notch; the Boston-White River Junction, Vermont *Cheshire*, and finally the Boston-Troy (Albany) New York *Minuteman*.

In the spring of 1957 the 2.75 million mile *Yankee* was retired and placed in the Edaville museum near Cape Cod, Massachusetts. Most recently, in 1993 she was disassembled and trucked to the Crawford Notch area of New Hampshire's White Mountains. Perhaps she once again will feel steel rails rolling under her wheels, and another gener-

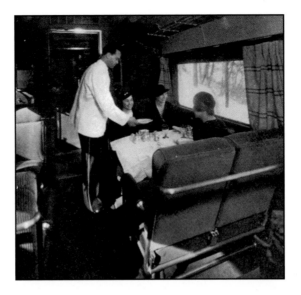

Both photos, Tom Pearson

Meal service for parties of three of four was by a table erected between swiveling seats. There were coat racks on the rear of seats and overhead racks for hats and parcels.

In the coach sections of the new Flying Yankee, *hand baggage was stowed above the seats as well as in a special compartment at the end of the car.*

AN OPPORTUNITY TO RIDE ON THE NEW "FLYING YANKEE"

After its exhibition tour of from two to three weeks on the Boston and Maine Railroad and the Maine Central Railroad, the new "Flying Yankee," in response to requests already received, will operate excursions to "nowhere" from various communities on both railroad systems. The round-trip fares on these excursions (runs of approximately 50 miles) will be $1 per passenger.

The dates of the excursions will be announced later, but you should make your reservations NOW with the agent at the nearest place to your home. The space on the train is limited.

It has already been tentatively planned to operate these "excursions to nowhere" from the communities listed below. Both railroads will, however, be glad to consider requests from service clubs or other organizations in other communities to run a "Flying Yankee" excursion. The new train cannot, however, operate from all stations on these "nowhere" excursion runs, as a track for turning it must be available within the excursion area.

Boston, Lynn, Salem, Fitchburg, Worcester, Greenfield, Springfield, Lawrence, Haverhill, Troy, N. Y.; Nashua, and Concord, N. H.; Biddeford, Portland, Lewiston, Auburn, Brunswick, Augusta, Waterville and Bangor, Me.

Make all requests to W. O. Wright, Passenger Traffic Manager, North Station, Boston, Mass.

Tom Pearson

At Old Orchard Beach, Maine, the Flying Yankee *arrives on time to unload and pick up waiting passengers who wanted to ride on the new deluxe stainless steel machine.*

FLYING YANKEE ARRIVING AT OLD ORCHARD BEACH, MAINE

Jay Christopher

36

ation of New Englanders will come trackside to admire her. One thing is clear, her stainless steel frame and roof purlins are just as square today as they were leaving Budd 60 years ago.

A MIDDLE AMERICA *ZEPHYR* DUET

Responding to the resounding success of its original *Zephyr*, the Burlington placed orders for two near duplicates, #9901-02. The deletion of the RPO section allowed the new *Twin Zephyrs* to seat 88 rather than 72 passengers.

Rolling off the line in spring, 1935 the *Twin Zephyrs* were introduced to the Chicago-Twin Cities trade with full-blown public relations hype. The Burlington was getting competition from the

The stainless steel Flying Yankee *lead unit sits in the Edward G. Budd plant undergoing final construction.*

The original Flying Yankee *remains intact in the 1990s in New England, awaiting possible renovation.*

BOSTON and MAINE

Don Heimburger

Don Heimburger

Slightly worse for wear, this is the stainless steel hulk of the 1935 lightweight diesel-electric *Flying Yankee. During the first year of operation, the train carried 94,524 passengers with revenues of $266,864. Traffic studies indicated that 48 per cent of the volume was new business.*

Don Heimburger

When the Yankee *began, it left Portland, Maine in the morning, ran to Boston, then made a roundtrip from Boston to Bangor followed by a Boston to Portland trip in the evening.*

The new Twin Zephyrs, according to promotion material, were "scientifically streamlined, cruise easily at 80 to 90 miles an hour and are capable of speeds well over 100."

This was part of an advertising brochure the Burlington printed to promote the Twin Zephyrs. Above is shown the cover of the brochure—at right was one of the inside pages.

HERITAGE FROM THE GODS
BURLINGTON'S *new 8 car* TWIN ZEPHYRS

ATTAINING SUBLIME HEIGHTS

Out of the fabled heritage from the gods, the Burlington has fashioned a brilliant new achievement in the art of travel—The 8-Car Twin Zephyrs.

Glorified in stainless steel are the power and wisdom of Jupiter, the metallurgy of Vulcan, the beauty of Venus, the handicraft of Minerva, the legendary virtues of a dozen deities, plus the supernal, silent speed of Pegasus and Zephyrus. Each shining car is a shrine to the god or goddess whose name it commemorates.

Superseding the spectacular three-car Zephyrs that established the first streamline train service between Chicago and the Twin Cities, each of these super-Zephyrs supplies commodious coach accommodations for 160 passengers, luxurious parlor and parlor-lounge cars, spacious dining facilities, and a convivial cocktail lounge.

The interior of each car is an individual color creation by the eminent architect, Paul Cret, who collaborated with Burlington engineers and the builders in consolidating the finest developments of art and science.

A Burlington heritage of 88 years of practical progressive railroading and more than five million miles of Diesel-powered train experience also is embodied in these Twin Zephyrs, whose gay interiors capture the spirit of their flashing speed, whose passenger appointments are as pleasing as their graceful exteriors.

Morning and afternoon in each direction, flashing along the scenic Mississippi River route over one of the finest stretches of railroad track in the world, these shining streamlined trains thrill Burlington passengers between Chicago and St. Paul and Minneapolis with new joys that the Zephyrs have brought to travel.

The Twin Zephyr *three-car trains were originally designed to operate on the basis of a single daily trip between Chicago and the Twin Cities. Two months after the initial run, however, in April, patronage had increased so that it was necessary to operate the* Twins *on daily roundtrip service, a total of 882 train-miles per day for each train. During the first year of service, the* Twins' *availability was 96.8 per cent.*

ULTRA-MODERN AIR-CONDITIONED STREAMLI

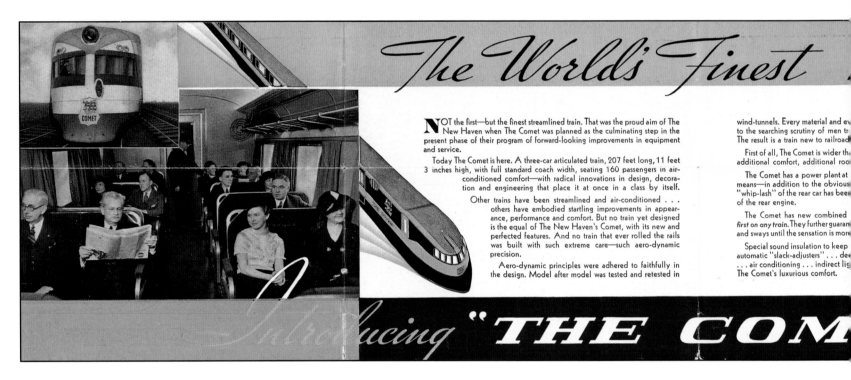

The World's Finest

NOT the first—but the finest streamlined train. That was the proud aim of The New Haven when The Comet was planned as the culminating step in the present phase of their program of forward-looking improvements in equipment and service.

Today The Comet is here. A three-car articulated train, 207 feet long, 11 feet 3 inches high, with full standard coach width, seating 160 passengers in air-conditioned comfort—with radical innovations in design, decoration and engineering that place it at once in a class by itself.

Other trains have been streamlined and air-conditioned . . . others have embodied startling improvements in appearance, performance and comfort. But no train yet designed is the equal of The New Haven's Comet, with its new and perfected features. And no train that ever rolled the rails was built with such extreme care—such aero-dynamic precision.

Aero-dynamic principles were adhered to faithfully in the design. Model after model was tested and retested in

wind-tunnels. Every material and ev to the searching scrutiny of men tr The result is a train new to railroad

First of all, The Comet is wider th additional comfort, additional roo

The Comet has a power plant at means—in addition to the obvious "whip-lash" of the rear car has bee of the rear engine.

The Comet has new combined first on any train. They further guaran and sways until the sensation is more

Special sound insulation to keep automatic "slack-adjusters" . . . de . . . air conditioning . . . indirect lig The Comet's luxurious comfort.

Introducing **"THE COM**

The New Haven railroad offered The Comet, *the last word in luxury rail travel with their Duralumin-built passenger train. "Not the first, only the finest streamlined train," offered the promotional materials.* The Comet *was to make the Boston to Providence trip (44 miles) in only 44 minutes.*

Chicago & NorthWestern and the Milwaukee Road for this market, so only the best would do. Enthusiasm was at a fever pitch when on April 14, 1935 #9901 ran from Chicago 38 miles to Aurora, Illinois with 44 sets of human twins to meet #9902. After suitable ceremony, the twins were split up and both *Zephyrs* ran side by side back to Union Station. Twin Cities service on a 6 1/2 hour schedule started the next week on April 21, 1935.

Business was so brisk that the original single one-way trip per train set was doubled beginning

June 3, 1935. This resulted in each set running off 882 miles per day, 7 days a week. Steam-hauled coaches would occasionally have to be substituted, but the *Twins* averaged 97% availability that first year and the sold out sign was a regular occurrence. They, too, grossed about four times the cost of operation.

By mid-year, 1936 the 3-unit *Twins* patronage had grown so much they worked themselves out of a job. Replaced by new 6-car trains, #9001 was reassigned to Dallas-Houston service as the *Sam Houston Zephyr* while #9002 became the *Ozark*

ED TRAIN .. THE NEW HAVEN'S "COMET"

STREAMLINED TRAIN

...used in the completed train was subjected technique of aero-dynamic engineering.

...ns of its type—by nine inches. This means h in aisles—as well as additional stability.

...two 400 horse power Diesel motors. This of full operation in either direction—that , thanks to the steadying weight and drive

...nd spring-resisting shock absorbers—*the* et's "ride"—damping out all tiny jolts, jars g than rolling...no matter what the speed.

. rubber mountings to absorb vibration ... s ... wide windows with draped curtains ese and other improvements contribute to

The genius of American industry collaborated in the construction. Goodyear-Zeppelin Corporation ... Aluminum Company of America ... Westinghouse Air Brake Company, and more than 100 other manufacturers ... all contributed their best talents in specifying, designing and manufacturing various materials and mechanical apparatus used in the construction. The Westinghouse Electric and Manufacturing Company supplied the Diesel engines, generators and motors, the electric lighting system, and the air-conditioning.

The Comet will supplement The New Haven's already celebrated fleet of trains on the "boulevard of steel", led by the Yankee Clipper and Merchants Limited, a fleet that provides air-conditioning on *every* day-train and includes fifty new-type streamlined day-coaches as regular equipment on through trains.

The Comet will be operated between Boston and Providence, making the 44 miles in 44 minutes including stop at Back Bay, without subjecting passengers to *excessive* speeds at any point in the run.

ET" ... last word in luxury rail travel

State Zephyr between St. Louis and Kansas City. They worked their miracle in Missouri and Texas as well. The #9901 was tragically destroyed in a grade crossing crash in 1944, but #9902 was honorably retired and scrapped in 1956.

A RAILBOUND COMET

Following closely on the heels of its New England neighbors, the New Haven embarked on a streamliner program to cut costs and boost patronage. Forsaking the traditional builders, and even newcomer Budd, New Haven placed its order for a 3-car bi-directional streamliner with

Goodyear Zeppelin. Like several other carriers, only receipt of a Federal WPA loan for $250,000 allowed the bankrupt New Haven to order this new train.

As a manufacturer of lighter-than-air craft, Goodyear was an expert in aluminum fabrication, which undoubtedly helped them snare the order.* They created a 3-section articulated bi-directional carbody. The *Comet* seated 106 passengers, was 11 feet 6 inches high and contained two 400 hp Westinghouse engines—one in each end. All carbody fabrication was of aluminum,

* An interesting alternative was the competitive bid from Budd, back-to-back shovelnoses articulated with two coaches. It never left the drawing board and was undoubtedly more expensive than Goodyear's bid.

The Burlington's Mark Twain Zephyr *was the fourth Burlington* Zephyr *train introduced, placed in service between St. Louis and Burlington, Iowa in October of 1935. The 221-mile route was covered, with 16 intermediate stops and nine flag stops, in 5 hours and 45 minutes.*

Mark Twain Zephyr along the Mississippi, Quincy, Illinois

Floor plan of The Comet *depicts the tubular construction in the outer shell, especially the nose. The train consisted of three body sections articulated and carried on four trucks. The final design was selected after a series of wind tunnel tests on models at the Daniel Guggenheim Airship Institute at Akron, Ohio and at Columbia University where a running belt was used to simulate the relative velocities between car bottom, air and tracks. The natural tone of the aluminum was augmented by a striking color scheme worked out, in collaboration with the New Haven, by the Sherwin-Williams Company which furnished the varnishes and enamels used for both interior and exterior finishes.*

with partially recessed rivets. Tubular construction meant the elimination of a center sill, a fabrication change which would resurface in NH's famous "American Flyer" cars, the first 50 of which were being built and delivered at this time.

Since the *Comet* was designed for short-haul service on the 44 miles between Boston and Providence, Rhode Island, amenities were rather plain. However, it sported mechanical air conditioning, indirect lighting, and deeply cushioned, rust-colored mohair walkover seats. The interior walls were brown, the drapes at the "picture windows" were complementary beige, and the pink tinted ceiling provided an excellent contrast. Miscellaneous interior trim and seat frames were aluminum.

After a month-long system tour, the *Comet* entered service June 5, 1935 on a five roundtrips per day basis. The 44-mile trip was scheduled for 44 minutes, and the non-stop 37.5 miles between Providence and Boston's Back Bay station required an average speed of 73.7 mph to remain on time. One hundred-mile-per-hour dashes between Attleboro and Sharon, Massachusetts, were the rule rather than the exception.

To mark her approach, the *Comet* had a vertical headlight mounted at each end as well as the normal one. Local lore recounts that on misty nights the reflected vertical shaft of light was visible for miles, long before even the rumble of the diesels was heard.

Like most of the other fixed consist trains,

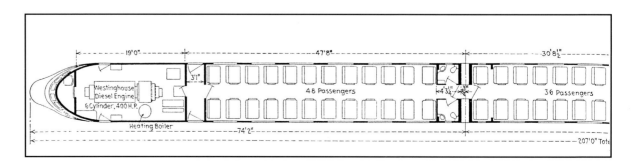

19'0" — 47'8" — 30'8½"

Westinghouse Diesel Engine 6 Cylinder, 400 H.P.

3'1"

48 Passengers

4'3½" · 8"

36 Passengers

Heating Boiler

74'2"

207'0" Total

"Out of the fabled heritage of the gods..." came these streamlined speedsters, each shining car a shrine to the god or goddess whose name it commemorated. The large headlights atop the power car alerted motorists of its approach.

Los Angeles Union Station, with the terminal annex post office in the rear, is highlighted in this early 1940s night scene. Costing $11 million, the station typified the charm and hospitality of southern California.

Inside Los Angeles' Union Station, the comfort and convenience of waiting passengers was taken into consideration. This view shows the lavish appointments of the Waiting Room, with leather upholstered settees, large chandeliers and large windows for the bright sun to light the room. The pastel colors were common schemes in this part of the country.

The massive front of Denver Union Station was of Modern Gothic Architecture, situated on the east side of the Platte River at the foot of 16th, 17th and 18th streets. Later additions carried to 15th Street. The original dimensions were 503 feet long and 65 feet wide, but numerous additions changed this. At one time a 165-foot tower built of volcanic tuff from Castle Rock, Colorado, graced the southeast corner. The first floor of the depot was devoted to passenger service, express service and mail; the second floor was used by various railroads for their offices.

Up to and during the Great Depression, Denver Union Station was the busiest place in Denver: hundreds of thousands of new arrivals passed through it to man the developing mines, pineries, industries and livestock ranges in the West, and recruits off to three wars said goodbye to family and friends in its spacious rooms.

WWII's patronage crush and gas rationing meant their replacement by standard steam-hauled consists, and up to 20 of those "American Flyer" semi-streamlined coaches of which Pullman-Standard ultimately supplied 205. After the war, *The Comet* was shifted around several Boston area commuter slots, and finally scrapped for its aluminum in July, 1952. Of course, its replacement was none other than the commonplace Budd car!

'FLEET OF FOOT WAS HIAWATHA'—*LONGFELLOW*

Not only fleet of foot, but of steel wheels as well. As the Milwaukee Road's premier service between the Twin Cities and Chicago, it had been conceived to counter both the Burlington *Zephyr* and the Chicago & NorthWestern *"400"* service. With company headquarters on line in Chicago, the local road had to fight back and did so with a vengeance. The *Hiawatha* ultimately carried the most passengers in perhaps the most hotly competitive rail passenger market in North America.

On May 29, 1935 the Milwaukee introduced its new, streamlined *Hiawatha* service. A short, 6-car consist of three coaches, lounge-diner and

Jay Christopher

The Hiawathas *of the Chicago, Milwaukee, St. Paul & Pacific Railroad linked together Midwest cities such as Chicago, St. Paul-Minneapolis and Omaha. Early* Hiawathas *featured steam locomotives sheathed in streamlining plates that covered the interworkings of the engine. The gray, orange and maroon paint scheme was striking, especially with the trailing cars.*

Called the Beaver Tail car, this Hiawatha *parlor car—shown in early 1935—was a unique and stylish passenger accommodation designed to attract the traveling public. No other U.S. road owned cars such as these. After this picture was taken, brass* Hiawatha *script was added below the windows. By November of that year, more than 100,000 passengers had ridden the* Hiawatha.

two parlors—one the famous "beaver tail" observation, initiated the service. Soon lengthened to nine cars, what the trains still lacked in length they made up for in panache and popularity.

Decor in the coaches and parlor cars included flesh colored ceilings, brown walls and green flooring, accented with aluminum trim. "Moderne" influence entered the dining car, with walnut wainscoting, stainless steel trim and olive green upholstery. However, the best was saved for the Tip Top Tap, which featured French grey flooring with orange stripes and walls of black with a similar orange wainscoting—highlighted by stainless steel trim.

If that weren't enough, the upper walls blended from deep lemon color to the ivory ceiling. The chrome-plated tubular chairs had orange leather seats. The bar—first on a train in North America—was, to quote sources of the day, "fully equipped and well stocked." Many passengers never found their coach seat after locating the Tap!

The "HI" was powered by four of the handful of 4-4-2 Atlantic-type steam locomotives built in the 20th Century. With drivers 84" in diameter, these Alco-built engines promptly and profitably propelled the "HI" into the record books. Legendary were the "slow to 90" speed boards on the Milwaukee, as the spiffy streamliner backed briefly away from the century mark (or better). Famous for its red/orange exterior and excellent timekeeping, *Hiawatha* service soon grew in both frequency and train length. By November, 1935 more than 100,000 passengers had boarded the "HI."

The Milwaukee Road, like many other Western-route railroads, promoted the national parks as a way to attract train riders. In this instance, Yellowstone National Park, a prime candidate for this promotion, is pictured as a beautiful, inspiring area to visit by rail.

THE HIAWATHA
CHICAGO, MILWAUKEE, ST. PAUL, MINNEAPOLIS
THE MILWAUKEE ROAD

The Hiawatha *was first powered by streamlined steam locomotives such as #2, a 4-4-2 Atlantic-type. The* Hiawatha *made its first trip on May 29, 1935.*

After a brief 16 months of service, the "HI" was totally re-equipped, with an express-tap car, full diner, three parlors and four coaches. Clearly, the Tip Top Tap lounge car was the most popular spot on the train, and its reputation equaled that of the most exclusive clubs in Chicago. With this re-equipping, the end car became a true observation, with rearward facing seating.

The lightweight steel cars were constructed by the railroad at its West Milwaukee shops. An additional bonus of riding the train was the knowledge that so doing was supporting the local railroad in these still difficult years.

We are pleased
to have you on board to join us in celebrating the

Twenty-fifth ANNIVERSARY of Hiawatha Service

On May 29th, 1935, the first Hiawatha Train was placed in service between Chicago and the Twin Cities.

Today we are turning back the clock twenty-five years, and the menu that we are offering you is typical of that which was offered our guests in 1935. The price of this meal is the actual charge that was made on that memorable occasion. We want you to enjoy your meal and, perhaps, it may bring back memories of your former travels.

Dinner

•

Sixty-five Cents

Consomme Clear
Hot or Cold

Choice of:

Grilled Lake Superior Whitefish
Lemon Butter

Lamb Chop - "Hiawatha"

Roast Young Chicken
au jus

Snowflake Potatoes

Demi Cut Wax Beans

Dinner Rolls

Fresh Berry Pie
Cheese

Ice Cream

The Cheese Crock

Coffee

Tea

Iced Tea

Milk

Egg Entree substituted upon request

This is the cover of the menu used in the dining cars of the original Hiawathas in 1935

Silver Anniversary Menu

The Super Dome Hiawathas

1935~1960

PENNSYLVANIA R.R. BURLINGTON ROUTE | THE ALTON ROAD | MILWAUKEE R.R.
UNION STATION

Ultimately, the speedy 4-4-2's put themselves out of work, as train weights exceeded their pulling capacity. In 1938 they were replaced by new 4-6-4 Baltic (Hudson) types, which could handle the now-standard 15- or 16-car consists. They were "speedlined by Otto Kuhler," as so autographed above the cylinders. Regardless, diesel power entered the picture in 1940, but its conquest would not be complete until after WWII. The *Hiawatha* fleet soon included various services, but the premier remained the *Morning* and *Afternoon Hiawathas*, which lasted for over a generation.

Designed by Daniel H. Burnham's architectural firm, Chicago's Union Station, at the corner of Canal and Adams streets, was officially opened on April 18, 1925. It took 12 years to build and cost $75 million, with a two-year delay because of World War I. The original station consisted of two structures: the Concourse Building and the headhouse, connected by an underground passage. The Waiting Room in the main building was inspired by the Roman baths of Carcacalla and Diocletian.

Lasting for over a generation, the Milwaukee Road's Hiawathas offered fast and luxurious train service between Chicago, Milwaukee, the Twin Cities and other major Midwestern points. The Milwaukee Road had begun researching the possibility of lighter weight trains as early as 1932. The Hiawathas were steam-powered until 1941 when the first diesel power was used, an EMC E6 which ran on Train #6, the eastbound Morning Hi.

Hiawatha Carries 4,968 Persons in 11 Days

The "Hiawatha," fast train of the Chicago, Milwaukee, St. Paul & Pacific, carried 4,968 revenue passengers in the first 11 days of operation. The best day's record was set on Saturday, June 8, 1935, when 335 revenue passengers were carried northbound and 328 southbound, or a total of 663. The average total northbound for the first 11 days was 222, while the southbound average was 231, a daily total of 453.   *-1935 news report*

To a legendary name is added a great record of achievement···

The Hiawathas

THE Milwaukee Road points pridefully to the record of its great fleet of HIAWATHAS. Improved again and again since the original was placed in service, these Speedliners were so soundly conceived and built that they have scarcely been marked by the huge traffic of the war years. Today's

HIAWATHAS are still tops in comfort, beauty, speed—and in patronage. Milwaukee Road trains now in the making will provide luxury and beauty that will lift passenger travel to a new high. Your vacation or business trips will pay dividends in comfort if you ride on one of the HIAWATHAS.

F. N. Hicks, Passenger Traffic Manager, Chicago 6, Ill.

HIAWATHAS SERVE CHICAGO · MILWAUKEE · NORTHERN WISCONSIN · MINNEAPOLIS
ST. PAUL · CEDAR RAPIDS · DUBUQUE · DES MOINES · OMAHA · SIOUX CITY · SIOUX FALLS

THE MILWAUKEE ROAD

The July 1, 1951 Milwaukee Road public timetable celebrated the past by showing steam, electric and earlier diesel locomotives on its cover (full cover not shown).

WARNING

The Pullman Company calls the attention of its patrons to the fact that "Card Sharks" and "Con Men" have started their winter campaign on railroad trains.

Passengers can protect themselves by refusing to play with strangers.

SAFETY FIRST LAST AND ALL THE TIME!

Chris Burritt

The beautiful dark blue, red and yellow Indian design of the Milwaukee food menu added elegance to the patron's dining pleasure. In this menu, a Manhattan or Martini was only 60¢.

The early years saw very low diesel production in the United States: between 1925 and 1936, 190 diesel-electric locomotives were produced by the major builders. In this advertisement, the American Locomotive Company tried to bridge the growing field of locomotion, offering to build steam, electric or diesel engines for their clients.

What do you feed an Iron Horse?

IT was easy to tell in the old days, when you could see the boiler and the smokestack and the steam whistle. You could tell at a glance you fed it coal and water.

But these modern, streamlined steeds—their stomachs hidden under sleek bodies of gleaming steel—what is it you feed them? Coal? Oil? Or electricity?

Actually, all three are used. For modern, functional railroading demands that a locomotive be powered for a specific job.

For some jobs, steam can't be beat. For others, Diesel is the answer. For still others, it's electricity.

That's why American Locomotive builds all three. We know from over a hundred years of experience that only a complete analysis of the conditions to be met can result in the right selection.

Today, a large percentage of America's crack passenger and freight trains are pulled by American Locomotive engines—

some steam, some Diesel, some electric. Each is unsurpassed at its particular job, for each was built for that particular job.

American Locomotive
NEW YORK

DIESEL   ELECTRIC   STEAM

Even Pullman helped lure passengers on board trains by using advertisements such as this Grand Circle plan which enticed travelers on a coast to coast tour, with Pullman as their home en route.

PORTLAND, OREGON'S NEW NAMESAKE

Confident long before the wildly successful promotional tour of the M-10000 had begun, the UP ordered a longer, larger train from Pullman even before the *City of Salina* was completed. Finished early in the fall of 1934, the new M-10001 consisted of a 900 hp power car; RPO-baggage; Pullmans *E.H.Harriman*, *Oregon Trail* and *Abraham Lincoln*; and a chair car/buffet. It could whisk 118 passengers along in stellar comfort.

Second of a series on Union Pacific train personnel

The Engineman

The man who operates the locomotive of a Union Pacific train has three primary duties—to handle his train safely, to handle it with the utmost comfort to its passengers, and to bring it in on time.

He *must* know his job for he has served successively as freight-train fireman, passenger-train fireman, and freight-train engineer, before being promoted to passenger engineer.

His engine too, deserves special mention. Designed by Union Pacific mechanical engineers, it is capable of amazingly long and continuous runs before being changed out for inspection. For example, the same locomotive runs through from Cheyenne, Wyo. to Huntington, Ore., nearly 900 miles.

Courtesy is a Habit on the Union Pacific

At left, the engineer holds an oil can in the days when steam was supreme on the rails. Taken from the November 9, 1930 Union Pacific public timetable.

Like its Budd counterparts, buffet meals were served at seats via seatback-mounted tray tables. Additionally, this streamliner was the first to contain Pullman sections, compartments and bedrooms. Pullman experimented with sliding aluminum panels to cover each section, giving extra privacy. However, like the M-10000, the streamliner had a narrower and lower cross-section than standard equipment and sides tapered inward from floor to ceiling. Aluminum trim was freely used to highlight the painted wall and ceiling surfaces.

Determined not to let the Burlington *Zephyr* get all the glory, the UP arranged a transcontinental speed run for its new streamliner. The M-10001 departed Los Angeles at 10 pm on October 22, l934 and reached New York City 56 hours and 55 minutes later. It averaged 57 mph for the 3,250 miles and once attained 120 mph. Crowds again flocked to stations along the train's route.

After its demonstration performance, the M-10001 returned to Pullman for several modifications. Its 900 hp V-12 engine was replaced with a 1,200 hp V-16 one, and a diner-lounge car was added to the consist. With these modifications, the M-10001 stretched 455' from nose to tail and weighed 265 tons, sans passengers. Interestingly enough, the additional car and new power plant

Pioneering in the introduction of streamlined trains for passenger service, the Union Pacific's M-10000 was tested in every sort of weather including snow, rain, wind, dust storms and cold.

59

The M-10001, the City of Portland, *established a transcontinental record on its demonstration tour when it completed 3,250 miles between Los Angeles and New York at an average speed of 57.2 miles per hour, breaking the previous record by 14 hours. The seven-car train weighed 265 tons.*

modifications did not increase its fare-carrying capacity at all. The UP spent the extra money to insure optimal timekeeping and maximum passenger satisfaction. It truly was a different era.

Finally, on June 6, 1935 the streamliner *City of Portland* settled down to a five-roundtrips-per-month schedule between Chicago and Portland. Each leg covered the 2,272 miles in 39 hours and 45 minutes. "Sailings" from Portland or Chicago were society column affairs, and the sold out sign

15827. Streamliner operating over Union Pacific System

Union Pacific's City of Los Angeles *began regular service on May 15, 1936 covering the 2,298 miles at an average speed of 57.8 mph. Pullman-Standard Car Mfg. built the cars, Electro-Motive Corp. made the engine and power plant, and General Electric supplied the electrical components.*

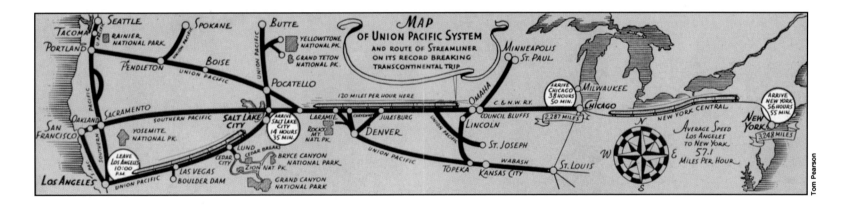

MAP OF UNION PACIFIC SYSTEM AND ROUTE OF STREAMLINER ON ITS RECORD BREAKING TRANSCONTINENTAL TRIP

Tom Pearson

was nearly always at hand. The first nine months of operation recorded 86,360 patrons.

SOMETHING BORROWED, SOMETHING BLUE AND PRESIDENTS REMEMBERED

As America's oldest, if not most conservative railroad, the Baltimore & Ohio proudly dated its heritage from the earliest days of the 1830s. Although in no way handling the passenger volume of its major competitor, the Pennsylvania, still the B&O had an ambiance all its own.

The City of Portland's *menu cover featured an overview of Portland, Oregon and mighty Mount Hood in the distance. By promoting cities, national parks and areas of interest along its right-of-way, the Union Pacific promoted passenger train travel.*

Portland, Oregon and mighty Mount Hood from an eminence west of the City, showing the business district divided by the Willamette River.

Streamliner

"CITY OF PORTLAND"

Passengers had a number of travel options when riding the B&O between Chicago and the East Coast. There was the Pittsburgh Express, the Chicago Express, the Shenandoah, the Capitol Limited, and others. In 1939, a coach fare between Chicago and New York City was $22.69, or between Chicago and Baltimore, $19.27.

Like most roads in the early 1930s, the B&O was staggering with passenger losses and nearly empty trains. As streamliner talk developed in the industry, Chief of Motive Power and Equipment George Emerson decided to look for himself.

On the basis of a $900,000 Federal RFC loan, in 1934 the B&O ordered two lightweight streamliners. One was constructed of aluminum, the other of lightweight Cor-Ten steel. American Car & Foundry produced the two 8-car sets, each consisting of a baggage-mail car, three reclining-seat coaches, one diner-lunch counter car, two parlor cars and a parlor-observation. Motive power was built in the company's Mount Clare Shops, a 4-6-4 *Lord Baltimore* and a 4-4-4 *Lady Baltimore*. Except for some wartime 4-8-2's, they were B&O's last new steam engines.

Each car interior was decorated in the finest of Eastern establishment conservatism. A mixture of brown carpet or linoleum, tan wall surfaces and ivory ceilings predominated. The seats in the smoker were upholstered in brown leather, while the remaining coaches and parlor seats were

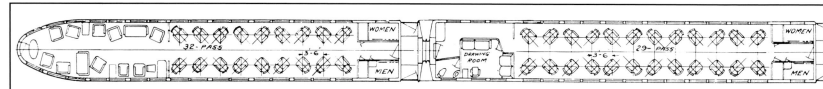

done in mohair plush. The only true dash of color was at the lunch counter, where the stool tops were covered with orange and black leather, and the sidewalls painted salmon. According to connoisseur Lucius Beebe, the coaches even had petitpoint antimacassars to keep the seatback fabric clean! Heavy upholstered chairs and mahogany side tables occupied the observation lounge. Its curtained windows shaded the mahogany writing table which held heavy gauge B&O-embossed stationary available for brief notes written "En Route."

B&O also had a reputation for excellent dining service. Whether in a streamliner, or an older heavyweight train, B&O meals were legendary. Long stemmed roses were present for luncheon and dinner, while the completed meal brought not only the check, but a fingerbowl as well.

Initially both new streamliners were planned for *Royal Blue* service between Jersey City (NYC) and Washington D.C. However, only the aluminum car set and 4-6-4 engine were assigned. The Cor-Ten steel cars and 4-4-4 were sent to the B&O-controlled Alton, where they were assigned

to Chicago-St. Louis service as the *Abraham Lincoln* on July 1, 1935.

On June 24, 1935 the streamlined *Royal Blue* was inaugurated. However, the most important addition to these trains arrived the following month: Electro-Motive's first separable passenger locomotive, B&O boxcab #50. Testing on both trains occurred until April 27, 1936 when #50 was permanently assigned to the *Abraham Lincoln*.

On April 27, 1936, the streamlined steam-driven Abraham Lincoln was replaced by a diesel-electric 1,800-horsepower unit. Below, the interior of the streamlined cars is shown in the sketch.

Reflecting New Principles in Streamlined Trains

BALTIMORE & OHIO—first railroad in the world to air-condition trains—will put into service on July 1 "The Abraham Lincoln"—

a new streamlined train to which new principles of construction and design have been applied. It is the first streamlined train to be operated by a steam locomotive, the first to be built of standard size cars and each car is an individual unit so that any car can be taken out of the train at any time or other cars added.

DESCRIPTION OF NEW TRAIN

In keeping with the modern vogue for color, the new streamlined train, including the locomotive, is painted a rich, royal blue.

The locomotive itself is unique. Its full weight is only 294,000 pounds. This compares with

400,000 pounds —the weight of the ponderous "Philip E. Thomas" locomotive which pulls the popular Capitol Limited over the mountain grades. It has 84-inch driving wheels to permit increased speed.

The new train consists of a locomotive and six cars; a combination Mail-Baggage Car; two Individual Reclining Seat Coaches; Parlor Car,

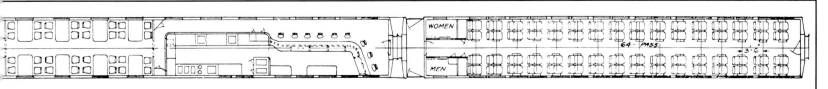

The Class DP-1, No. 50 was built by Electro-Motive, for the Baltimore and Ohio, and was the first self-contained diesel passenger locomotive in the U.S. It is now on display at the Museum of Transport in St. Louis.

In April of 1936 the B&O No. 50, an 1,800-hp B-B type locomotive, was permanently assigned to the Abraham Lincoln. *Here she leaves Chicago's Union Station.*

COURTESY

A Baltimore & Ohio Tradition

YOUR railroad ticket reads that it is good for one continuous passage to your destination. Beyond that, you rightfully expect a comfortable seat or berth, a well-ventilated car, a smooth roadbed, and the efficient, punctual service of a modern railroad.

To this the Baltimore & Ohio adds a heaping measure of courtesy—a courteous, thoughtful attention that comes from a genuine "will to please"—a desire to make you feel at home while aboard our trains—a spirit calculated to assure your utmost comfort and contentment.

This old-fashioned courtesy, we believe, is an outstanding mark of our service—a real Baltimore & Ohio tradition.

Baltimore & Ohio

Conservative B&O forever holds the honor of operating the first diesel-electric streamliner consisting of full sized, separable, non-articulated cars.

In 1937 the B&O purchased Electro-Motive's first passenger E unit (so named for its "E"ighteen hundred horsepower). There is perhaps nothing more synonymous with the Streamliner Era than Electro-Motive's six-axle, brightly painted, rounded nose units. Ironically, the B&O never really was comfortable with lightweight streamliners and only purchased one more set, the *Columbian* of 1947. The 1935 *Royal Blue* equipment was sent to the Alton and renamed the *Ann Rutledge* and likewise placed in Chicago-St. Louis service.

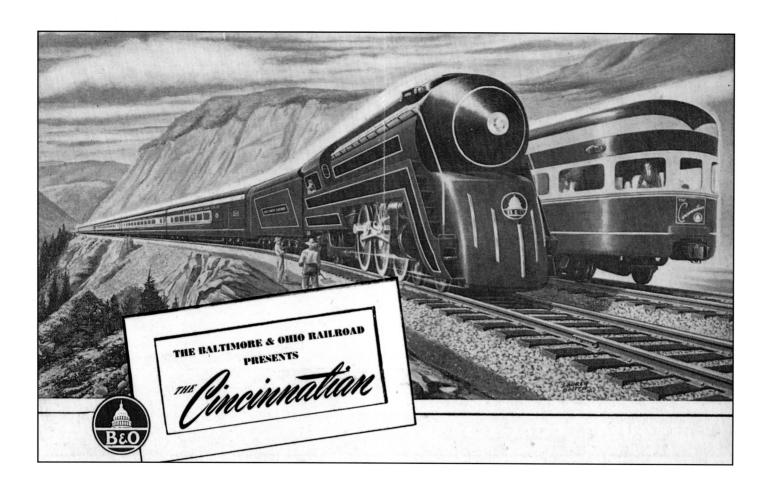

THE BALTIMORE & OHIO RAILROAD
PRESENTS
The Cincinnatian

B&O

The first deluxe, all-coach, daylight streamliner between Baltimore, Washington and Cincinnati was the well-known Cincinnatian. *It was painted in blue, gray and silver, and streamlined from front to rear.*

Showing its mix of avant garde and conservatism, the B&O retained Otto Kuhler to style its *Royal Blue* of 1937. It rolled out in retro-fitted heavyweight splendor behind a President's Class 4-6-2 Pacific, complete with Kuhler's trademark bullet nose and firebox skirts. The rebuilt heavyweight equipment held sway on the *Royal Blue* until its discontinuance in 1958. Even more striking, the soon-replaced-by-diesels 4-6-2 was de-streamlined and put back to work in the regular pool. Amazingly, it would be re-streamlined after WWII for service on the *Cincinnatian*. Few steam engines were streamlined—even fewer got a second chance.

THE REBEL'S YELL OR ... BURBLE

In a year which saw an incredible diversity of streamlined equipment developed, perhaps the Gulf, Mobile & Northern's *Rebel* was unique. The two, 226' long, 3-car non-articulated sets included a power-RPO-baggage car, a divided or "Jim Crow" buffet-coach and a sleeper-observation. Overnight service was between Jackson, Tennessee and New Orleans via Jackson, Mississippi.

The *Rebel* was one of only two early streamliners to be powered by Alco and contained an inline 6-cylinder 600 hp engine. Fabricated of Cor-Ten steel by American Car & Foundry, the little train shared the use of mid-car vestibules with its early articulated counterparts. The reason was segregation, not articulation. The colored section was coach only and had no access to the buffet grill. Likewise, the first class observation-lounge and sleeping compartments were white only.

**FOR MORE
COMFORT—THRIFT—SAFETY**

Travel by train

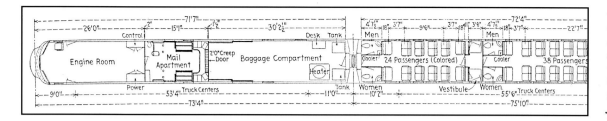

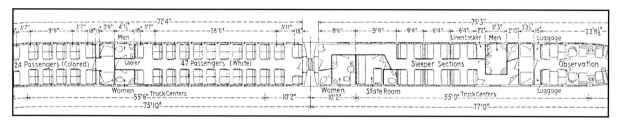

Completely replacing steam locomotives for passenger trains, the Gulf, Mobile & Northern's Rebel(later the Gulf, Mobile & Ohio) was a three-car non-articulated train set that ran between Jackson, Tennessee and New Orleans via Jackson, Mississippi. It was the first streamliner in the South.

The use of full-width diaphragms and full length underbody skirts gave the impression of a single articulated train. The *Rebel* was a sharp sight with its silver body highlighted by the grey car skirts and red window band. Streamlining was designed by none other than Otto Kuhler of Milwaukee *Hiawatha* fame.

Air conditioning was a highly promoted feature of this Deep South streamliner, but its features didn't stop there. Interior colors such as ivory, mocha, rust and slate grey were intermingled for maximum effect across the train's seating areas. Tufted leather chairs, venetian blinds, indirect lighting and the first recorded use of train hostesses also helped boost patronage. Indeed, over 40% of *Rebel* patrons claimed to have been enticed out of their cars.

Since traffic was heavier between New Orleans and Jackson, a fourth coach served that market. It was short-cycled off the northbound train and added to the southbound during regular operation. In 1937 a third equipment set was added to extend service to Meridian, Mississippi as well. The little *Rebels* ran through the mid-1950s and are still fondly remembered in the rural Deep South.

By the summer of 1935, the limitations of the early streamliners with their fixed consists and integral power units had become abundantly clear. New equipment ordered after July, 1935 consisted of separable cars and locomotives, or a mixture of articulated car sets with independent locomotives. The little *Rebel* of the GM&N, like the previously discussed B&O equipment, was a member of this coming second generation of streamliners. It had taken all of 15 or so months for the designers of Budd, Pullman-Standard, Electro-Motive and Alco to move into second generation equipment. The trial period of the articulated streamliner thus closed, with fanfare, profit and an even brighter tomorrow.

ABOARD THE REBEL

Gulf, Mobile & Ohio streamliners speed daily between St. Louis and Mobile, and Jackson, Tennessee and New Orleans, traversing the beautiful Gulf South.

The Mobile Rebel has through Pullman service to and from Chicago. GM&O was America's first railroad to have hostesses on streamliners. *Promotional copy.*

"THE REBEL"—GULF, MOBILE & OHIO STREAMLINER, JACKSON, TENN.—33

Jackson is a city of mild climate. The fact that the community is literally in the middle of West Tennessee serves to make it headquarters for trade, recreation and entertainment for the vast number of persons living within its recognized trade territory. The Gulf, Mobile & Ohio operates air-conditioned, streamlined trains between Jackson, New Orleans and Mobile to the south, Jackson and St. Louis to the north. *Printed on rear of postcard.*

A Fertile Field

With the Santa Fe into the streamliner fray, competition began to heat up. The Santa Fe was a rail giant not to be underestimated.

The phenomenal impact early streamliners had on a Depression-demoralized America cannot be overemphasized. The passing flash of bright colors or stainless steel, the beautiful interiors and the income their creation produced, all assist-ed America toward recovery from the Depression.

So successful were those 1934-35 streamliners that this new mode of rail transportation was quickly accepted as profitable, safe and glam-

orous. The limitations of articulated equipment were realized, and meant most new equipment would be individual cars or locomotives, or perhaps at most a single articulated car set. Orders poured in to EMC, Budd, ACF and Pullman at such a rate that a backlog developed, and "Help Wanted" signs reappeared for the first time since 1929. The great pre-war competitions were at hand.

A SUPER FLEET LED BY
THE *SUPER CHIEF*

On May 12, 1936 in Chicago's Dearborn Station, the sire of perhaps the most famous of all American streamliners was born. Not a terribly unusual occurrence during the era, except that it was concocted of six standard Pullmans and nary a stainless steel or lightweight car was in sight! Five days before, the final articulated streamliner, Illinois Central's *Green Diamond*, began her Chicago-St. Louis career, but a major step in streamliner evolution was taking place—literally across town.

Aware of both the tremendous opportunity the new streamliners presented and of rival Union Pacific's commanding lead, Santa Fe ordered a 9-car stainless steel streamliner from Budd on April 14, 1936. Simultaneously, it freshened up six Pullmans from the regular equipment pool, and with great fanfare announced a new addition to its Santa Fe family. Not since the pre-WWI *De Luxe*, touted as "Extra Fine, Extra Fast and Extra Fare," had the traveling public been exposed to such a Santa Fe promotion.

Months before the public announcements, while the Burlington and UP were developing their articulated speedsters, on June 22, 1934 Santa Fe contracted with Electro-Motive to build and deliver two 1,800 hp passenger boxcab diesels. It likewise contracted with Budd to deliver a full-sized stainless steel passenger car, totally interchangeable with any other car on the ATSF roster. Both engines arrived in mid-1935, followed by ATSF #3070 in January, 1936. All were subjected to extensive testing. Indeed, #1 and #1A supposedly hit the 150 mph mark numerous times during various speed testing, some 30 years before electric powered test trains did so on the Northeast Corridor.

If the first *Super Chief* consist was traditional,

certainly the power was not. Growling at the head of this fledgling speedster was a new twin-unit diesel locomotive, of which only five existed. Two were owned by builder EMC, and the other by B&O. Never mind that rarity, the other box-cabs looked positively dowdy in comparison to the Santa Fe version.

In a bid to help break with railroading's past, EMC/GM offered customers the design services of its Detroit-based automotive styling department. Santa Fe likewise retained industrial designer Sterling McDonald, whose credentials included interior design work for the UP's two streamliners and Boeing's DC-3. As Santa Fe's press release stated, their diesels wore "a Cobalt Blue roof above a Scarlet stripe surmounting an Olive Green body based with a Tuscan Red stripe and deep Sarasota Blue undercarriage." McDonald threw in the illuminated purple *Super Chief* logo on both the locomotive and observation car for good measure. Patrons were going to notice this new "Super" *Chief* (the *Chief* had been ATSF's premier Chicago-Los Angeles train since 1926).

Thus *Super Chief* #1 rolled out of Dearborn Station that raw May night, a true transition train and nosed toward Los Angeles. It was carded at 39 hours, 45 minutes. Arrival would be under the

Odd-looking boxcab 1,800-hp diesels, arriving on the Santa Fe in mid-1935, took over the motive power duties on the luxurious Super Chief. Both locomotives #1 and #1A hit the 150-mph mark numerous times during speed testing.

74

ABOVE. The Santa Fe's twin diesel units were built by the St. Louis Car Company and featured shrouded front and rear ends to make them look streamlined. The units were powered by two 12-cylinder Vee 201A engines. Together the units contained 3,600-hp for the Chicago to Los Angeles extra-fare run of the Super Chief.

From the September 8, 1935 Santa Fe timetable, this promotion invited travelers to come to New Mexico or Arizona for relaxation, fun and air-conditioned comfort on the railroad's passenger trains.

Santa Fe Meal Service
(Management Fred Harvey)

The dining-car, dining-room, and station hotel service of the Santa Fe is managed by Fred Harvey. All through passenger trains, which do not carry dining-cars are scheduled to stop at dining stations, placed at convenient points along the line, and indicated in time tables thus—©. Ample time is allowed for meals.

Luncheon and Dinner for trains enroute are served table d'hote ($1.00 for adults and 75 cents for children occupying seats at the table). Breakfast 75 cents, except that service at Chicago, El Paso, Galveston, Houston, Kansas City, Lamy and Wichita is a la carte.

Dining-car meals are served a la carte, except that dinner on trains Nos. 3 and 4 and 23-24 (California Limited and Grand Canyon Limited) is optional, either a la carte or table d'hote.

Below is given a list of stations at which dining-rooms and lunch rooms will be found.

DINING ROOMS Seating Capacity	DINING ROOMS Seating Capacity	DINING ROOMS Seating Capacity	DINING ROOMS Seating Capacity
Albuquerque, N.M. 120	Chicago, Ill.,	Hutchinson, Kan. ... 110	*Seligman, Ariz. 86
Amarillo, Tex. ... 72	(Dearborn Sta.) ... 79	Kansas City, Mo. ... 104	*Syracuse, Kan. ... 104
*Arkansas City, Kan....... 88	Clovis, N.M. ... 98	*Kingman, Ariz. ... 63	*Temple, Tex. ... 65
*Ash Fork, Ariz. ... 120	*Colorado Springs, Colo.. 38	La Junta, Colo. ... 76	*Trinidad, Colo. ... 102
*Bakersfield, Calif. ... 72	Dodge City, Kan. ... 118	Lamy, N.M. ... 12	*Vaughn, N.M. ... 80
Barstow, Calif. ... 111	El Paso, Tex. ... 69	*Las Vegas, N.M. ... 68	*Waynoka, Okla. ... 56
*Belen, N.M. ... 64	Emporia, Kan. ... 104	*Merced, Calif. ... 56	*Wellington, Kan. ... 72
Brownwood, Tex. ... 62	*Ft. Worth, Tex. ... 24	Needles, Calif. ... 142	*Williams, Ariz. ... 72
*Canadian, Tex. ... 56	Gallup, N.M. ... 108	*Purcell, Okla. ... 52	*Winslow, Ariz. ... 124
*Chanute, Kan. ...	Grand Canyon, Ariz. ... 150	San Bernardino, Cal. ... 100	

*Temporarily closed.

LUNCH ROOMS Seating Capacity	LUNCH ROOMS Seating Capacity	LUNCH ROOMS Seating Capacity	LUNCH ROOMS Seating Capacity
Albuquerque, N.M. 124	Colorado Springs, Colo.......47	*Kingman, Ariz................42	Seligman, Ariz....................47
Amarillo, Tex....................51	*Deming, N.M................35	La Junta, Colo................64	Slaton, Tex......................46
*Arkansas City, Kan. 30	Dodge City, Kan. 47	Lamy, N.M. 34	Somerville, Tex. 50
Ash Fork, Ariz................62	El Paso, Tex................43	*Las Vegas, N.M. 51	*Sweetwater, Tex. 43
*Bakersfield, Calif..............47	Emporia, Kan. 44	Los Angeles, Calif. 48	Syracuse, Kan. 51
Barstow, Calif.................52	Ft. Worth, Tex. 38	*Merced, Calif. 32	*Temple, Tex. 20
Belen, N.M. 45	Gainesville, Tex. 42	*Mojave, Calif. 56	Topeka, Kan. 45
Brownwood, Tex...............33	Gallup, N.M................81	Needles, Calif................104	*Trinidad, Colo. 28
*Canadian, Tex................38	Galveston, Tex. 66	Newton, Kan................99	Vaughn, N.M. 42
*Chanute, Kan. 31	Grand Canyon, Ariz. 120	*Purcell, Okla. 20	Waynoka, Okla. 37
Chicago, Ill.,	*Guthrie, Okla................34	*Rincon, N.M. 30	Wellington, Kan. 67
(Dearborn Sta.) 34	Houston, Tex. 91	San Bernardino, Cal. 69	Wichita, Kan. 77
*Cleburne, Tex................42	Hutchinson, Kan............48	*San Diego, Calif. 41	Williams, Ariz. 53
Clovis, N.M. 54	Kansas City, Mo.............486	*San Marcial, N.M............20	Winslow, Ariz. 124

*Temporarily closed.

Guest Rooms	Guest Rooms	Guest Rooms	Guest Rooms
Albuquerque, N.M..... 120	Gallup, N.M. 64	Needles, Calif. 25	Temple, Tex. 21
Ash Fork, Ariz........ 21	Grand Canyon, Ariz.... 92	Rincon, N.M. 11	Trinidad, Colo. 22
Barstow, Calif. 29	Hutchinson, Kan. 80	San Marcial, N.M..... 7	Vaughn, N.M......... 4
Clovis, N.M........... 35	La Junta, Colo. 38	Seligman, Ariz. 19	Wellington, Kan....... 8
Dodge City, Kan...... 41	Lamy, N.M. 8	Somerville, Tex. 20	Williams, Ariz. 39
Emporia, Kan......... 7	Las Vegas, N.M. 37	Syracuse, Kan. 15	Winslow, Ariz. 69

At those hotels operated on the European plan the rates for rooms are generally $2.00 a day and up. Those operated on the American plan are $5.00 a day and up, except at El Tovar, where the rate is $7.00 to $9.00 a day and up.

The most noteworthy of the Santa Fe hotels are:

	Capacity Of Dining Rooms	Number of Guest Rooms
THE BISONTE, at Hutchinson, Kansas	110	80E
EL VAQUERO, at Dodge City, Kansas	118	41E
THE SEQUOYAH, at Syracuse, Kansas	104	15E
THE GRAN-QUIVIRA, at Clovis, New Mexico	94	35E
THE CARDENAS, at Trinidad, Colo	102	22E
THE CASTANEDA, at Las Vegas, New Mexico	108	37E
EL ORTIZ, at Lamy, New Mexico	9	8E
THE ALVARADO, at Albuquerque, New Mexico	127	120A&E
EL NAVAJO, at Gallup, New Mexico	112	64E
LA POSADA, at Winslow, Arizona	120	69E
THE FRAY MARCOS, at Williams, Arizona	62	39E
EL TOVAR, at Grand Canyon, Arizona	150	92A
THE ESCALANTE, at Ash Fork, Arizona	120	21E
EL GARCES, at Needles, California	152	25E
THE CASA DEL DESIERTO, at Barstow, California	110	29E

E—European Plan   A—American plan.

A 1934 Santa Fe timetable includes this list of Fred Harvey dining room and hotel services. By 1880 the English-born Fred Harvey had a deal with the Santa Fe to open restaurants along their right-of-way from Chicago to the West Coast. For more than 70 years Harvey Houses were known as the standard of first class dining throughout the Southwest. Harvey Girls, as they were known, dressed in white and black uniforms, were the waitresses who fed travelers, and during the 1940s, the troops in World War II. The Santa Fe's slogan was "Meals by Fred Harvey."

Within the advertisement:

She came in on the
Super Chief

How else would she travel to and from California?
For the Super Chief is one of the most glamorous all-room trains
in America, filled with people who know how to travel and
appreciate the best in travel.
It serves those famous Fred Harvey meals.
It operates on a 39¾-hour schedule between Chicago and Los Angeles.
The Super Chief is the flag-bearer of Santa Fe's fine fleet of
Chicago-California trains which run each day.

SANTA FE SYSTEM LINES... Serving the West and Southwest
T. B. Gallaher, General Passenger Traffic Manager, Chicago 4

Santa Fe

"She just came in on the Super Chief" was the thing to say when the Super Chief *was the way to travel. The glamorous train carried hundreds of important people and movie stars.*

fabled California sun, with Engineer Galard Sloanaker posing by Hollywood star Eleanor Powell holding a bouquet of roses. Thus was reinforced an association between Santa Fe and Hollywood that reached legendary proportions over the next three decades. During those pre-jet years, "just got in on the *Super*" was an expression known and used as frequently as possible in business, social and Hollywood circles.

Sleek, trim and adorned with the Santa Fe's Warbonnet livery, #8 was delivered from EMC in 1938; these units were the first in a long line of E-type diesels built by EMC for the railroad.

As the weekly *Super* #1 rolled across the ATSF system, the streamlined *Super Chief* developed at Budd and EMC. At La Grange, an artist in EMC's Streamlined Train Department developed its new

The Santa Fe Promotions Department liked to show its passenger trains traveling to warm climates and exotic locations in the Southwest and the West. Promotions like this helped bring Midwesterners out West, and kept the road's passenger trains full.

This color rendering was produced by the General Motors Art and Colour-Industrial Design Department in the mid-1930s to depict how Santa Fe's new diesel E units would look.

Donald Duke

paint scheme. The story is best recounted by Stan Repp in his magnificent tribute *Super Chief, Train of the Stars*: "..Wearing a green celluloid eye shade, artist Leland A. Knickerbocker, 43, hunched over a large drawing table. Knickerbocker, book-illustrator turned train-illustrator, had before him the rakish perspective of what could well have been an elongated automobile.

"Dipping a no. 7 brush into a puddle of crimson poster paint at the edge of his butcher-pan palette, Knickerbocker rendered the nose of that automobile-like shape, actually the hood of Super-2's own diesel. ...A narrow band of that red color ran the length of both units at floor height suggesting, as Knickerbocker said, 'The profile of an Indian head and the trailing feathers of a war bonnet.'"*

*SUPER CHIEF, Train of the Stars, Stan Repp, 1980; Golden West Books.

79

Thus was modestly born the Santa Fe Warbonnet paint scheme, internationally known and still in use today, some 60 years after Knickerbocker put brush to paper. Of all the railroad paint schemes developed over the years, only neighboring Union Pacific with its yellow and grey has such a long lasting corporate image.

While EMC welded, and Budd Shotwelded, the architectural talents of Philadelphians Paul Cret and John Harbeson were being brought to bear on the interior of *Super* #2. Using Navajo Indian designs provided by the Santa Fe, and a wood veneer called Flexwood, the *Super* soon had an interior like none other.

The observation car had window pier panels with Navajo Indian designs painted on cork to imitate the original sand paintings. Seat fabrics were woven—not printed—Indian designs, with an occasional dropped stitch for that hand-woven effect. The Flexwood paneling covered virtually every horizontal or flat surface remaining, sans the deeply carpeted floors. Rosewood, holly, maple, redwood burl, teak, satinwood and others graced these beautiful cars in both public and private accommodations.

Finally, in late April, 1937 the 9-car streamlined *Super Chief* rolled out of Budd and onto a siding for interchange and delivery to the Santa Fe. The train consisted of an RPO-storage mail car, mail-baggage car, four sleepers, lounge, diner and sleeper-observation. A total of 104 passengers and a crew of 12 could be accommodated behind #2A-B, the streamlined diesel-electric locomotive.

A marching band, radio announcer and assorted hoopla were all present on the evening of May 18, 1937 when *Super* #2 left Dearborn Station for the first time with a full complement of passengers. Food, drink, manicure, even a shave were all available to the privileged, pampered and duly ensconced travelers. The *Super* was worthy of carrying the mantle of Santa Fe's finest.

The June 11, 1939 Santa Fe timetable named the three heavily-traveled Santa Fe trains: Super Chief, Chief *and the* El Capitan.

DL-109/DL-110 Nos. 50 and 50A were built in 1940 for the Santa Fe by the American Locomotive Company. The twin units developed 4,000 hp and weighed 326 tons.

FLAG BEARERS OF AMERICA'S LARGEST FLEET OF STREAMLINED TRAINS

Super Chief • *The* Chief El Capitan

THE SUPER CHIEF

There is now twice-a-week service on this tremendously popular and ONLY SOLID PULLMAN, 39¾-hour, extra fare streamliner between Chicago and Los Angeles. Departures are from Chicago, Tuesdays and Saturdays 7:15 p. m.; from Los Angeles, Tuesdays and Fridays 8:00 p. m.

THE CHIEF

The Chief, consists of beautiful new equipment streamlined in stainless steel, now as modern as the Super Chief—thus further emphasizing the distinction of this finest, fastest and only extra-fare Chicago-California DAILY train. Leaves Chicago 12:01 p. m. daily; leaves Los Angeles 11:30 a. m. daily.

EL CAPITAN

The only all-chair-car, 39¾-hour transcontinental streamliner in America! It saves days and dollars and lifts economy travel to a plane of luxury never before offered to coach passengers. El Capitan leaves Chicago Tuesdays and Saturdays at 5:45 p. m.; Los Angeles Tuesdays and Fridays at 1:30 p. m.

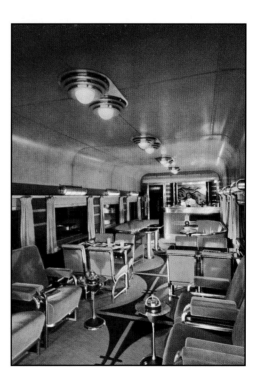

A description of the dining car *Cochiti* on that first evening would go like this: white linen tablecloths complemented the ATSF Mimbreno Indian china and heavy sterling silver flatware. The floor was carpeted in a brown/red block pattern and the chairs covered in an orange/red fabric. Window shades were yellow with a grey stripe, and the drapes the color of desert sand. A single rosebud was centered on each table, and the built-in walnut-covered buffet was centered below a mirror of peach-tinted glass. Walls were African rosewood and indirectly lighted by fluorescent tubes. All this before dinner, which would be of equal splendor and quality.

Out of a fleet of 16 streamliners, the Santa Fe's extra-fare Super Chief *and* Chief *were the flagbearers.*

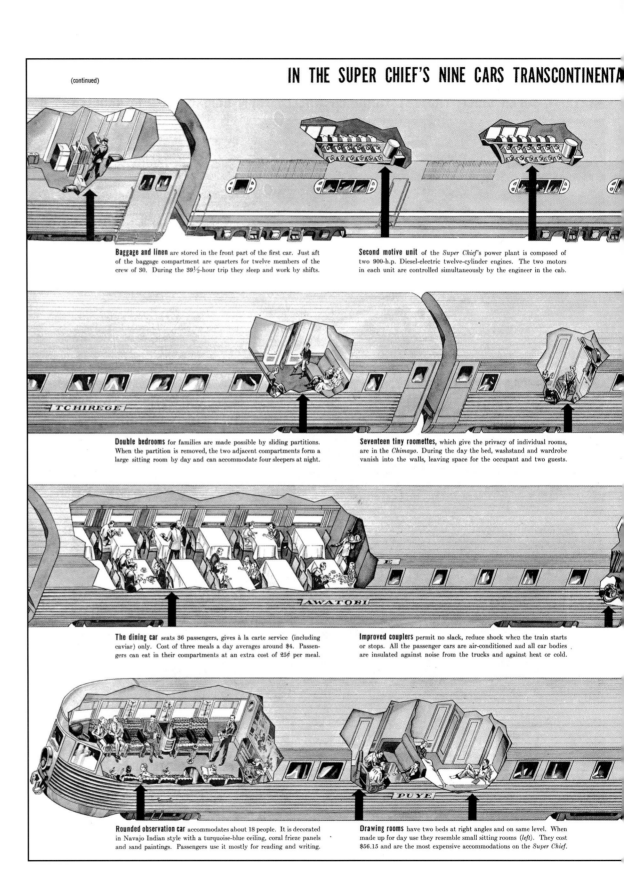

Baggage and linen are stored in the front part of the first car. Just aft of the baggage compartment are quarters for twelve members of the crew of 30. During the $39\frac{1}{2}$-hour trip they sleep and work by shifts.

Second motive unit of the *Super Chief's* power plant is composed of two 900-h.p. Diesel-electric twelve-cylinder engines. The two motors in each unit are controlled simultaneously by the engineer in the cab.

Double bedrooms for families are made possible by sliding partitions. When the partition is removed, the two adjacent compartments form a large sitting room by day and can accommodate four sleepers at night.

Seventeen tiny roomettes, which give the privacy of individual rooms, are in the *Chimayo*. During the day the bed, washstand and wardrobe vanish into the walls, leaving space for the occupant and two guests.

The dining car seats 36 passengers, gives à la carte service (including caviar) only. Cost of three meals a day averages around $4. Passengers can eat in their compartments at an extra cost of 25¢ per meal.

Improved couplers permit no slack, reduce shock when the train starts or stops. All the passenger cars are air-conditioned and all car bodies are insulated against noise from the trucks and against heat or cold.

Rounded observation car accommodates about 18 people. It is decorated in Navajo Indian style with a turquoise-blue ceiling, coral frieze panels and sand paintings. Passengers use it mostly for reading and writing.

Drawing rooms have two beds at right angles and on same level. When made up for day use they resemble small sitting rooms (*left*). They cost $56.15 and are the most expensive accommodations on the *Super Chief*.

TRAVELERS FIND EVERY FORM OF HOTEL COMFORT

The locomotive is also powered by twin 900-h.p. Diesels. They operate generators which make electricity which runs motors geared direct to the axles of the six-wheel trucks, producing a high traction power.

Engineer is perched high at the front of the spick-and-span cab. It is insulated against both outside and inside noises, thereby making it easier for the engineer and assistant to exchange signal observations.

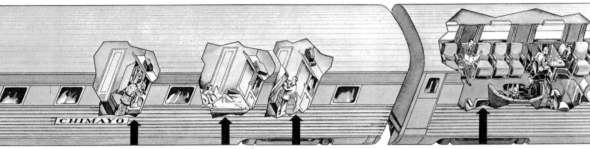

Three positions of roomette furniture are shown above. When dressing, occupant pulls out washstand, opens wardrobe. At night the bed occupies most of compartment. Morning, passenger raises bed against wall.

A passenger lounge is at rear end of the baggage-lounge car. Passengers sit and chat in heavily upholstered chairs and settees. The color scheme ranges from dark red on walls to light gray-blue on the ceiling.

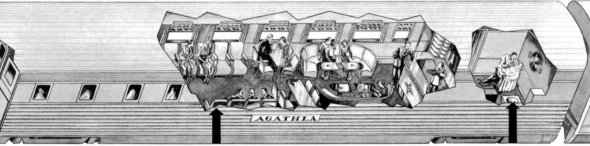

Cocktail lounge has modern furniture made of square metal tubing with molded rubber seat cushions, covered with woven fabric. Two tables are arranged for card players. Barman serves drinks at any hour of trip.

Barbershop is a useful asset to any transcontinental train as most passengers don't like to shave while moving at 80 m.p.h. Next to the barbershop is a shower room. The train crew sleeps at other end of car.

Compartments on the *Super Chief* are larger than the roomettes and more expensive. Roomettes cost $22.05; compartments sell for $39.50. All the windows on the new streamliner are shaded by Venetian blinds.

Section sleeper comprises eight sections. Cheapest fare includes the cost of an upper berth at $12.60; lower berths cost $15.20. If you want to buy an entire section for yourself you must pay an additional $10.

Attractions on board the Super Chief included double bedrooms for families, a passenger lounge with heavily upholstered furniture and settees, a diner seating 36 passengers or passengers could eat in their compartments, a cocktail lounge with barman, a barbershop and shower room, and a rounded observation car seating 18 in comfort.

"For economy travel's greatest thrill," read the promotional piece on the El Capitan, the all-chair transcontinental streamliner. The train made the 2,000-mile-plus trip in 39 hours and forty-five minutes.

Soft, warm interior tones that vary from car to car relieved the monotony of the traveler's surroundings. Old rose combined with lake red, buff and tans; stainless steel and chrome trim; olive and grey greens, orchid and composing shades; side walls feature wood veneer and carpeted floors. Santa Fe did it right!

The Fastest
MOST CONVENIENT SERVICE EVER OFFERED
CHICAGO
SPRINGFIELD
ST. LOUIS

4 hrs. 55 MINUTES

The GREEN DIAMOND

America's smoothest riding train provides the fastest service ever offered between Chicago and St. Louis. Traveling northbound, you can leave St. Louis in the morning after breakfast . . . enjoy a full afternoon in Chicago for business or pleasure . . . and be back in St. Louis the same evening. Southbound you can leave Chicago at the end of the business day and be in St. Louis at a conveniently early hour the same evening.

Luxurious comforts en route—air-conditioned luxurious coaches and parlor car . . . low priced meals . . . stewardess-registered nurse . . . radio . . . reserved seats and *No Extra Fare.*

SOUTHBOUND				NORTHBOUND	
5:00 p.m.	Lv.		Chicago—Central Station	Ar.	1:50 p.m.
5:07 p.m.	Lv.		53rd Street—Chicago	Ar.	1:43 p.m.
5:10 p.m.	Lv.		63rd Street—Chicago	Ar.	1:39 p.m.
8:02 p.m.	Ar.		Springfield—Adams St.	Lv.	10:43 a.m.
9:55 p.m.	Ar.		St. Louis	Lv.	8:55 a.m.

LUXURIOUS EQUIPMENT
The equipment of all 3 of Illinois Central's passenger trains between Chicago and St. Louis is the finest possible. Complete air-conditioning in all cars including the new Illinois Central luxury coaches—the last word in comfort for coach travel. Travel between St. Louis and Chicago is a real pleasure via Illinois Central.

LOW PRICED MEALS
Illinois Central's dining car "Meals Supreme" make any journey more enjoyable. Delicious economy meals served to coach passengers on the Green Diamond, the Daylight and the Night Diamond. Tasty wholesome Breakfasts may be had for only 25c, Lunches 35c, Dinners 40c. Also low priced table d'hote and a la carte service.

LOW FARES
Low fares are in effect everywhere, every day, on Illinois Central trains. Only 2 cents a mile in coaches, 3 cents a mile in parlor or sleeping cars. Lower for round-trip.

5½ hrs

The DAYLIGHT
NEW More Convenient Schedules

11:35 a.m.	Lv.	Chicago	Ar.	5:45 p.m.	
3:00 p.m.	Ar.	Springfield	Lv.	2:14 p.m.	
5:05 p.m.	Ar.	St. Louis	Lv.	12:15 p.m.	

FASTER SERVICE TO TEXAS AND THE SOUTHWEST
This fine train leaves Chicago just before noon and arrives in St. Louis in time to make convenient connections with fast trains for Texas, Mexico and the Southwest, leaving St. Louis at 5:30 P. M. Northbound from the Southwest, Mexico and Texas excellent connecting service is offered by the Green Diamond leaving St. Louis at 8:55 A. M.

POPULAR OVERNIGHT

The DIAMOND

This de luxe train leaves at midnight, giving you a full evening in Chicago. A restful sleep on a comfortable train and an arrival in St. Louis at a convenient morning hour.

11:55 p.m.	Lv.	Chicago	Ar.	7:30 a.m.	
4:30 a.m.	Ar.	Springfield	Lv.	2:40 a.m.	
7:18 a.m.	Ar.	St. Louis	Lv.	12:05 a.m.	

ILLINOIS CENTRAL
The Road of Cordial Service

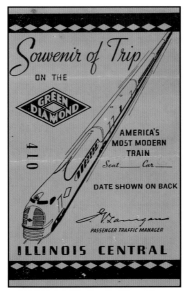

After only nine months, on February 22, 1938 the *Super Chief* schedule was made twice weekly and the new equipment now included private showers for each set. The latest *Super Chief* was complemented by the 5-car *El Capitan*, a coach-only train, but complete with diner and observation car. A similar, 6-car coach streamliner called the *San Diegan* linked its namesake city to Los Angeles later that year. The *San Diegan* soon acquired the RPO-storage mail car built for the original Budd *Super Chief* of 1937. All including the fabled daily *Chief* were now stainless steel streamliners, thanks to the delivery of more than 130 cars from Budd and Pullman. Although the trains were always full, daily *El Cap* and *Super* service would have to wait unit the end of WWII.

Illinois Central called it "America's Most Modern Train," and it included new spring suspension, modern roller bearings, stewardess-registered nurse on board and indirect lighting. "The diner-lounge-observation car is a marvel of modern beauty. Luxurious lounging chairs. Radio. Latest magazines. Modern kitchen with dry-ice refrigeration."

The Green Diamond, with
fully articulated five cars,
was painted dark green and
a lighter shade of green with
aluminum and scarlet
accents. Some called the train
the tomato worm; the train
stood taller than most others
of the time and weighed 230
tons.

HAIL AND FAREWELL: IC'S GREEN
INTERCITY CATERPILLER

Ordered on the strength of the Union Pacific's
phenomenal success with the *City of Salina*
and *City of Portland* streamliners, the Illinois Central's *Green Diamond* reprised the prewar articulated streamliner for its final time. By delivery on
March 27, 1936 the concept of total articulation
was already passe', but the *Diamond* was a fitting
closing monument to that brief, successful era.

Built by Pullman-Standard, the riveted 5-car aluminum worm was destined to spend its career in
service between Chicago and St. Louis. Looking
something akin to a seasick *City of Salina*, the
IC's first—and only articulated—motor train contained a baggage-RPO, dinette seating and coaches. On May 17, 1936 it began its daily 588-mile
single roundtrip between the two cities.

It was no accident that the *Green Diamond*
showed a family resemblance to the first two UP
streamliners. UP held a significant amount of IC
stock, and W. Averill Harriman sat on its board of
directors. Not only was the UP-Pullman image
quite understandable, but the GM automotive
influence of the mid-1930s showed with that
unmistakable huge, chrome grill and raised cab.

The *Green Diamond* was certainly not one of
the greatest success stories of the era, although it
did run for 10 years. Indeed, it wrapped up a
short, but vital part of the Streamliner saga, while
the Santa Fe *Super Chief* was starting the second
era across town in Chicago's Dearborn Station.
UP was already well ensconced at CNW's North
Western Station.

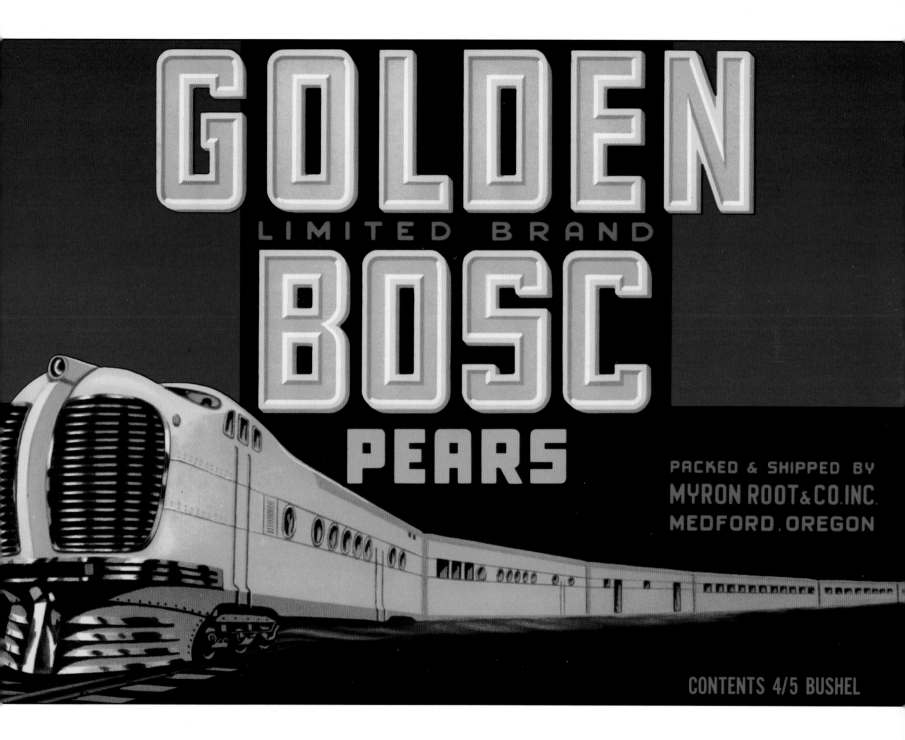

GOLDEN
LIMITED BRAND
BOSC
PEARS

PACKED & SHIPPED BY
MYRON ROOT & CO. INC.
MEDFORD, OREGON

CONTENTS 4/5 BUSHEL

UNLIMITED POWER:
THE *CITY* FLEET ARRIVES

As the inventor—at least in its own mind—of the American streamliner, the UP was not about to cede its position of leadership to anyone. It had notable competitors, specifically the Santa Fe in the Chicago-Los Angeles market, the Burlington for the Chicago-Denver trade, and even sometimes partner, sometimes competitor, SP on the Chicago-San Francisco Overland Route. Still, UP

Other companies besides railroads appreciated the dramatic styling of the early streamliners. This pear crate label is a prime example.

The Union Pacific's City of San Francisco *was also sponsored by the Chicago & NorthWestern and Southern Pacific. Begun in June of 1936, the train covered the Chicago to San Francisco run in 39 hours, 45 minutes.*

intended to dominate *all* the above markets, and other adjacent ones, as soon as equipment and opportunity permitted.

In the summer of 1935 UP ordered from Pullman twin EMC-powered, semi-articulated 9-car aluminum streamliners for both the Los Angeles and San Francisco to Chicago trade. Containing all the finery that any traveling movie star, businessman or executive could want, the threat of this Yellow Spectre was what made Santa Fe premier its original *Super Chief* on May 12, 1936. The day after the first *Super Chief* arrived in Los Angeles, its UP rival entered service.

Running on an equally hot 39 hour, 45 minute schedule to Los Angeles, this rolling hotel traveled via Omaha, Cheyenne (with a Denver connection) and Ogden. Its capacity of 84 Pullman plus 82 coach passengers was filled on its five-roundtrips-per-month service even with a surcharge of $5.00 in coach and $10.00 in sleeper. Demand was such that within months of its May 15, 1936 introduction, a second, 17-car train was ordered from Pullman.

On June 14, 1936 a nearly identical 9-car *City of San Francisco* entered service, also covering the distance between Chicago and the City by the Bay in 39 hours, 45 minutes. Service west of Odgen, Utah over Donner Pass to Oakland was provided by partner SP. All *City* trains used Chicago & NorthWestern trackage between Council Bluffs, Iowa and Chicago's NorthWestern station.

On December 22, 1937 Pullman and EMC delivered the new and improved *City of Los Angeles* to rave reviews. Behind its three diesels totalling an amazing 5,400 hp could be found a passenger conveyance with all the extras. Bedrooms, compartments, roomettes, open or enclosed sections, drawing rooms, duplex single rooms, and of course, coach seats were available, as well as barber, stenographer, hair stylist and that ultimate status symbol, the shower.

Perhaps most popular with frequent travelers was the *Little Nugget*, aka the bar car. It seated 35 patrons in a reproduction of Bonanza bordello finery. Flocked wallpaper, velvet drapes, marble tables and lace curtains created a stunning effect. Some claimed they never left the car, from their ticket lift until arrival at Los Angeles.

The Great Salt Lake at sunset provided a mystical background for this Southern Pacific postcard. Postage for the card "if salt bag attached with message, 3¢; without message, 1¹/₂¢."

Jay Christopher

The three City of Los Angeles *diesels totalled 5,400 hp when delivered in December 22, 1937, along with passenger cars with all the extras.*

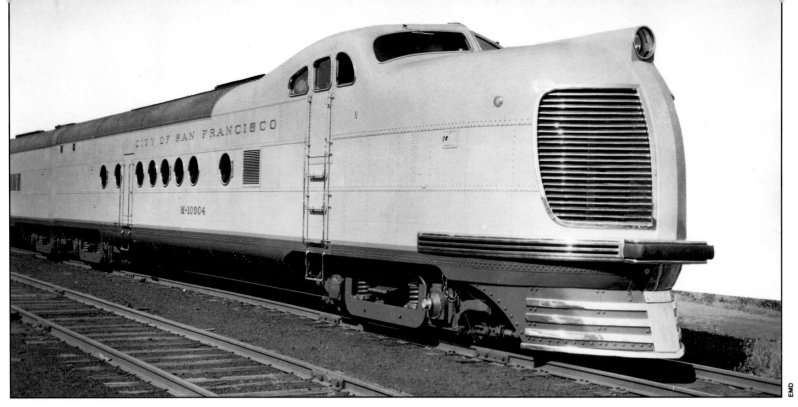

ABOVE: City of San Francisco.

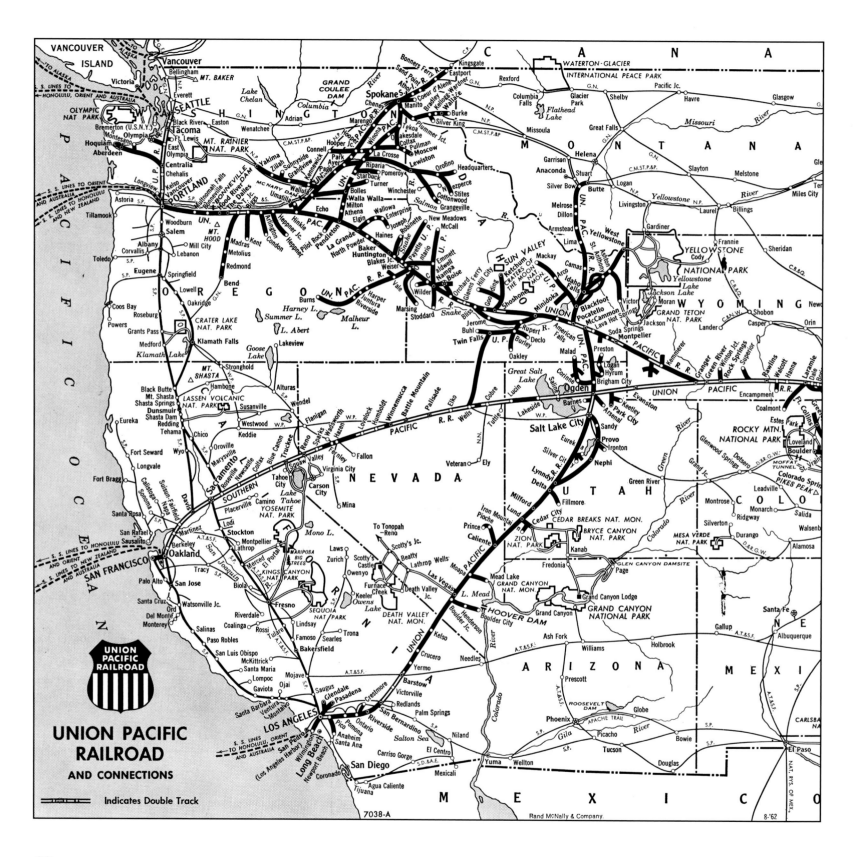

UNION
PACIFIC
RAILROAD

UNION PACIFIC RAILROAD

AND CONNECTIONS

━━━━━━ Indicates Double Track

7038-A   Rand McNally & Company.   8-'62

92

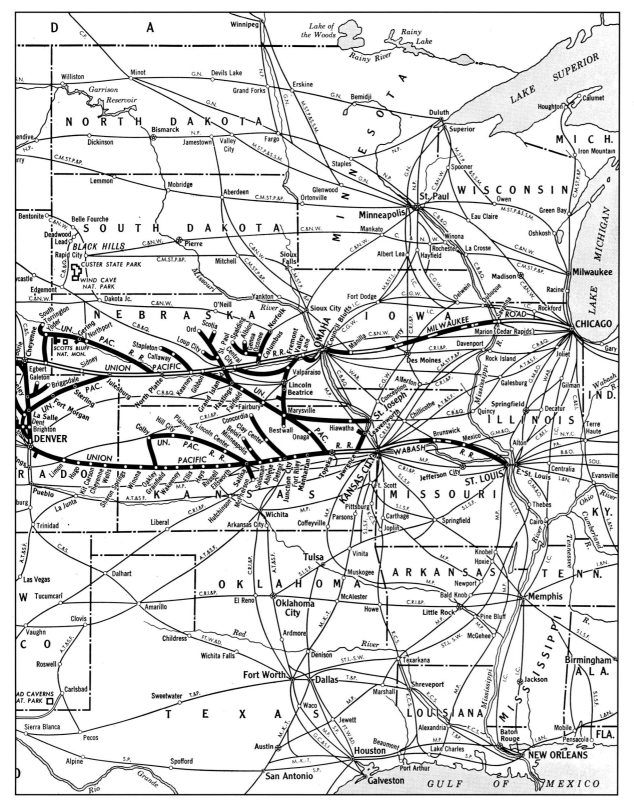

Union Pacific's western route included hundreds of miles of double tracked main line west of Omaha. UP's route was a natural thoroughfare which in early days had been followed by herds of buffalo, by Indians, traders, explorers, gold seekers, Overland Stage coaches and the Pony Express.

If the *Little Nugget* was absent from the consist, first class passengers could wander back to the portholed *Copper King* lounge observation for rest and relaxation. The circular windows contained Polaroid adjustable polarized non-glare glass, quite the innovation at the time.

In acknowledgement of the liquid foibles shared by many of Hollywood's finest, the *Hollywood* lounge seated 30 in moderne styling. Walls were covered in grey and white Formica, while seats were upholstered in scarlet nylon. The portholed windows were glazed in non-glare Polaroid glass. After cocktails, patrons could order the "Chef's Masterpiece" in the companion 56-seat dining car.

Products such as nylon, Polaroid and Formica were as new and exciting as *Gone with the Wind* was at the box office in 1939. The *City* apologized to no one on her weekly travels.

To start the new year, on January 2, 1938 the 17-car *City of San Francisco* joined the UP family and released the original set for other work. This time, however, UP exacted a price for the successes of the *City* fleet. The *City of Los Angeles* had equipment purchased on a percentage basis with Chicago & NorthWestern, and joint ownership of the *City of San Francisco* included the SP as well.

The *City* fleet was spectacular. *The City of San Francisco* featured a twin-unit diner stretching 144 feet, which contained a kitchen, 32-seat coffee shop and main dining room seating 64. The interior was painted in shades of blue, with complementing rust colored chairs.

The atmosphere for evening cocktails aboard the *City of San Francisco* was on par with the premier supper clubs of Chicago or San Francisco. Dormitory-club *Embarcadero* held 28 seats

EMD

and was panelled in fine woods. A mural fronted the round bar.

Tragically, on August 12, 1939 the westbound *City of San Francisco* derailed and crashed, likely the victim of sabotage. If true, the culprit or culprits were never caught, but their actions left eight passengers and 15 crew members dead, 11 cars of the train derailed and at least four totally destroyed. The twin-unit dining-kitchen cars were nearly demolished in the 60 mph crash, and their wreckage buried under the trailing cars. Most of the victims were crew members cleaning up in those two cars. Had it been earlier in the evening, when perhaps one third of the 149 passengers on board had been in those two cars, the fatalities would have been much higher.

While the unsuccessful manhunt continued, the UP began repairs to the damaged equipment and placed new orders with Pullman. The influx of new equipment was such that by early 1941 both the *City of Los Angeles* and *City of San Francisco* went from 5 to 10 trips per month service. The schedule remained unchanged until the post-war era, although wartime saw the removal of all full lounge cars and lengthening of running times.

Although the *Cities* were making reams of copy and plenty of money for the UP, they were not alone in UP's streamliner category. The increasing demand for space on the initial *City* sets gave UP and Pullman the chance in July, 1937 to provide an 8-car, all-Pullman train called the *Forty Niner* for alternate service to the five-times-monthly *City of San Francisco*. The Pullmans carried such names as *Bear Flag* and *California Republic,* and its dining car *Angel's Camp* was reputed to be on par with Delmonico's. Evidentally *Angel's Camp* had initially been ordered for

Gleaming in bright yellow paint, the City of San Francisco *streamlined locomotives were powerful and graceful.*

95

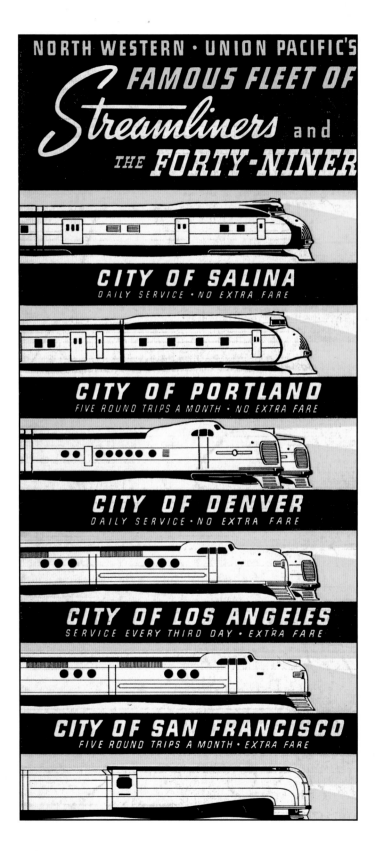

NORTH WESTERN · UNION PACIFIC'S
FAMOUS FLEET OF
Streamliners and
THE FORTY-NINER

CITY OF SALINA
DAILY SERVICE · NO EXTRA FARE

CITY OF PORTLAND
FIVE ROUND TRIPS A MONTH · NO EXTRA FARE

CITY OF DENVER
DAILY SERVICE · NO EXTRA FARE

CITY OF LOS ANGELES
SERVICE EVERY THIRD DAY · EXTRA FARE

CITY OF SAN FRANCISCO
FIVE ROUND TRIPS A MONTH · EXTRA FARE

In 1939 the Union Pacific was promoting six of its most fashionable trains with a separate timetable showing departure and arrival times, car consists and interior car arrangements. Said Union Pacific, "All of these fine trains are completely air-conditioned, splendidly equipped...provide the excellent personal service and delicious meals for which Overland Route trains are famous."

Cuban President Gerardo Machado, but Fulgencio Batista forced him out of office in 1933 before Pullman could deliver it. Presumably Batista's move was greatly appreciated by the train's patrons. For power, UP 4-8-2 steam locomotive #7002 was especially streamlined with a yellow and brown bathtub shroud in the Omaha shops. The tail sign was carried on a Pullman-supplied articulated duplex sleeper-lounge-observation.

The advent of the 1939-40 Golden Gate Exposition in San Francisco increased first class patronage on the Overland Route such that another streamliner was added, the *Treasure Island Special*. Also all-Pullman and steam powered, by the second year of service, the train was equipped with new sleepers of identical design to those just delivered for the *20th Century* and *Broadway Limited*. The 1933 *George M. Pullman* sleeper-observation carried the tail sign.

Meeting the *Cities*, and both the *Forty Niner* and *Treasure Island Special* at Cheyenne, was a short two- or three-car connecting train for Denver area passengers. Its Pullman-built aluminum coach-observation was that 1933 sibling of the *George M. Pullman*. With the end of the fair and more *City* equipment delivered, the *Treasure Island Special* faded into memory in the fall of 1940, and the *Forty Niner* followed on July 21, 1941.

Union Pacific service to Denver annoyed the Burlington, which considered Denver to be within its Western fiefdom. Boldly, the UP placed its sleeper-equipped and partially articulated equipment in service to the Burlington's hometown.

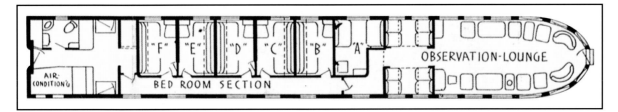

Double Bed Room—Observation Lounge Cars operate in the two Streamlined "City of Denver" (Illustrated), and the "Forty Niner." Full Length Observation Lounge Cars, with every new feature, are carried on both Streamliners, "City of Los Angeles," and on the Streamliner, "City of San Francisco."

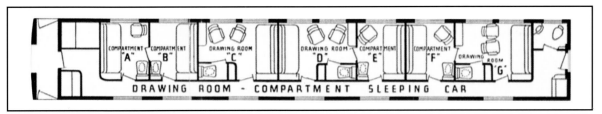

Type of Drawing Room and Compartment Sleeping Cars carried in the 17-car Streamliners, "City of San Francisco," and "City of Los Angeles."

The Streamliner CITY OF SAN FRANCISCO

WESTBOUND Read Down   **EASTBOUND Read Up**

Same Sailing Dates Each Mo.	Stream-liner No. 101	Extra Fare	Stream-liner No. 102	Same Sailing Dates Each Mo.
		C. & N. W. ⊙		
5 11 17 23 29	6.15	Lv **CHICAGO** (C.T.)............Ill. Ar	9.30	4 10 16 22 28
5 11 17 23 29	8.22	Lv Clinton....................Iowa Ar	7.15	4 10 16 22 28
5 11 17 23 29	9.38	Lv Cedar Rapids.............Iowa Ar	5.58	4 10 16 22 28
5 11 17 23 29	11.31	Lv Boone..................Iowa Lv	4.05	4 10 16 22 28
6 12 18 24 30	1.51	Ar **OMAHA**................Neb. Lv	1.45	4 10 16 22 28
		Union Pacific		
6 12 18 24 30	2.00	Lv **OMAHA**................Neb. Ar	1.35	4 10 16 22 28
6 12 18 24 30	4.01	Lv Grand Island............Neb. Lv	11.30	3 9 15 21 27
6 12 18 24 30	5.55	Ar **NORTH PLATTE** (C.T.)....Neb. Lv	9.44	3 9 15 21 27
6 12 18 24 30	4.56	Lv **NORTH PLATTE** (M.T.)....Neb. Lv	8.43	3 9 15 21 27
6 12 18 24 30	6.40	Lv Sidney..................Neb. Lv	6.59	3 9 15 21 27
6 12 18 24 30	8.25	Ar **CHEYENNE**.............Wyo. Lv	5.33	3 9 15 21 27
6 12 18 24 30	8.35	Lv **CHEYENNE**.............Wyo. Ar	5.23	3 9 15 21 27
6 12 18 24 30	10.00	Lv Laramie.................Wyo. Lv	4.03	3 9 15 21 27
6 12 18 24 30	11.47	Lv Rawlins.................Wyo. Lv	2.03	3 9 15 21 27
6 12 18 24 30	1.58	Lv Green River.............Wyo. Lv	11.50	3 9 15 21 27
6 12 18 24 30	3.45	Lv Evanston................Wyo. Lv	10.08	3 9 15 21 27
6 12 18 24 30	5.20	Ar **OGDEN** (M.T.)..........Utah Lv	8.35	3 9 15 21 27
		Southern Pacific		
6 12 18 24 30	4.30	Lv **OGDEN** (P.T.)..........Utah Ar	7.25	3 9 15 21 27
7 13 19 25 31	1.11	Ar Reno...................Nev. Lv	10.25	2 8 14 20 26
7 13 19 25 31	5.35	Ar Sacramento..............Cal. Lv	5.50	2 8 14 20 26
7 13 19 25 31	7.04	Ar Berkeley................Cal. Lv	4.26	2 8 14 20 26
7 13 19 25 31	7.12	Ar Oakland (16th St.)........Cal. Lv	4.17	2 8 14 20 26
7 13 19 25 31	7.50	Ar **SAN FRANCISCO** (P.T.)....Cal. Lv	3.45	2 8 14 20 26

THE FORTY NINER Streamlined Steam Train

WESTBOUND Read Down   **EASTBOUND Read Up**

Same Sailing Dates Each Mo.	Forty Niner No. 49	All Pullman — Extra Fare	Forty Niner No. 48	Same Sailing Dates Each Mo.
		C. & N. W. ⊙		
2 8 14 20 26	9.30	Lv **CHICAGO** (C.T.)............Ill. Ar	1.35	7 13 19 25 ⚹
2 8 14 20 26	12.14	Lv Clinton....................Ia. Ar	10.53	7 13 19 25 ⚹
2 8 14 20 26	1.44	Lv Cedar Rapids...............Ia. Ar	9.21	7 13 19 25 ⚹
2 8 14 20 26	4.15	Lv Boone...................Ia. Lv	6.55	7 13 19 25 ⚹
2 8 14 20 26	7.20	Ar **OMAHA**................Neb. Lv	3.50	7 13 19 25 ⚹
		Union Pacific		
2 8 14 20 26	7.35	Lv **OMAHA**................Neb. Ar	3.35	7 13 19 25 ⚹
2 8 14 20 26	10.12	Lv Grand Island............Neb. Lv	1.00	7 13 19 25 ⚹
3 9 15 21 27	12.37	Ar **NORTH PLATTE** (C.T.)....Neb. Lv	10.40	6 12 18 24 30
2 8 14 20 26	11.45	Lv **NORTH PLATTE** (M.T.)....Neb. Lv	9.33	6 12 18 24 30
3 9 15 21 27	2.07	Lv Sidney..................Neb. Lv	7.30	6 12 18 24 30
3 9 15 21 27	4.15	Ar **CHEYENNE**.............Wyo. Lv	5.45	6 12 18 24 30
3 9 15 21 27	4.25	Lv **CHEYENNE**.............Wyo. Ar	5.35	6 12 18 24 30
3 9 15 21 27	6.02	Lv Laramie.................Wyo. Lv	4.08	6 12 18 24 30
3 9 15 21 27	8.24	Lv Rawlins.................Wyo. Lv	1.48	6 12 18 24 30
3 9 15 21 27	11.15	Lv Green River.............Wyo. Lv	11.12	6 12 18 24 30
3 9 15 21 27	1.22	Lv Evanston................Wyo. Lv	9.07	6 12 18 24 30
3 9 15 21 27	3.25	Ar **OGDEN** (M.T.)..........Utah Lv	7.15	6 12 18 24 30
		Southern Pacific		
3 9 15 21 27	2.40	Lv **OGDEN** (P.T.)..........Utah Ar	6.02	6 12 18 24 30
4 10 16 22 28	1.35	Ar Reno...................Nev. Lv	7.08	5 11 17 23 29
4 10 16 22 28	6.35	Ar Sacramento..............Cal. Lv	2.03	5 11 17 23 29
4 10 16 22 28	8.35	Ar Berkeley................Cal. Lv	12.21	5 11 17 23 29
4 10 16 22 28	8.47	Ar Oakland (16th St.)........Cal. Lv	12.12	5 11 17 23 29
4 10 16 22 28	9.25	Ar **SAN FRANCISCO**.........Cal. Lv	11.40	5 11 17 23 29

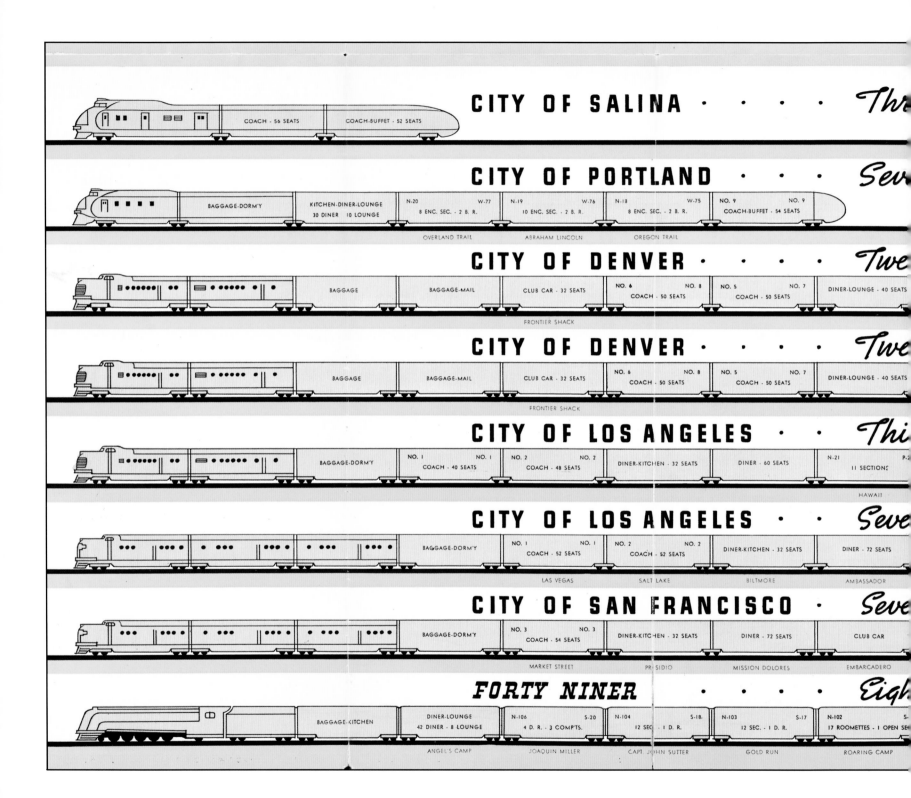

CITY OF SALINA · · · · _Thr_

COACH - 56 SEATS | COACH-BUFFET - 52 SEATS

CITY OF PORTLAND · · · _Sev_

BAGGAGE-DORM'Y | KITCHEN-DINER-LOUNGE 30 DINER 10 LOUNGE | N-20 W-77 8 ENC. SEC. - 2 B. R. | N-19 W-76 10 ENC. SEC. - 2 B. R. | N-18 W-75 8 ENC. SEC. - 2 B. R. | NO. 9 NO. 9 COACH-BUFFET - 54 SEATS

OVERLAND TRAIL · ABRAHAM LINCOLN · OREGON TRAIL

CITY OF DENVER · · · · _Twe_

BAGGAGE | BAGGAGE-MAIL | CLUB CAR - 32 SEATS | NO. 6 NO. 8 COACH - 50 SEATS | NO. 5 NO. 7 COACH - 50 SEATS | DINER-LOUNGE - 40 SEATS

FRONTIER SHACK

CITY OF DENVER · · · · _Twe_

BAGGAGE | BAGGAGE-MAIL | CLUB CAR - 32 SEATS | NO. 6 NO. 8 COACH - 50 SEATS | NO. 5 NO. 7 COACH - 50 SEATS | DINER-LOUNGE - 40 SEATS

FRONTIER SHACK

CITY OF LOS ANGELES · · _Thi_

BAGGAGE-DORM'Y | NO. 1 NO. 1 COACH - 40 SEATS | NO. 2 NO. 2 COACH - 48 SEATS | DINER-KITCHEN - 32 SEATS | DINER - 60 SEATS | N-21 P-2 11 SECTIONS

HAWAII

CITY OF LOS ANGELES · · _Seve_

BAGGAGE-DORM'Y | NO. 1 NO. 1 COACH - 52 SEATS | NO. 2 NO. 2 COACH - 52 SEATS | DINER-KITCHEN - 32 SEATS | DINER - 72 SEATS

LAS VEGAS · SALT LAKE · BILTMORE · AMBASSADOR

CITY OF SAN FRANCISCO · _Seve_

BAGGAGE-DORM'Y | NO. 3 NO. 3 COACH - 54 SEATS | DINER-KITCHEN - 32 SEATS | DINER - 72 SEATS | CLUB CAR

MARKET STREET · PRESIDIO · MISSION DOLORES · EMBARCADERO

FORTY NINER · · · · _Eigh_

BAGGAGE-KITCHEN | DINER-LOUNGE 42 DINER - 8 LOUNGE | N-106 S-20 4 D. R. - 3 COMP'TS. | N-104 S-18. 12 SEC. - 1 D. R. | N-103 S-17 12 SEC. - 1 D. R. | N-102 S- 17 ROOMETTES - 1 OPEN SE

ANGEL'S CAMP · JOAQUIN MILLER · CAPT. JOHN SUTTER · GOLD RUN · ROARING CAMP

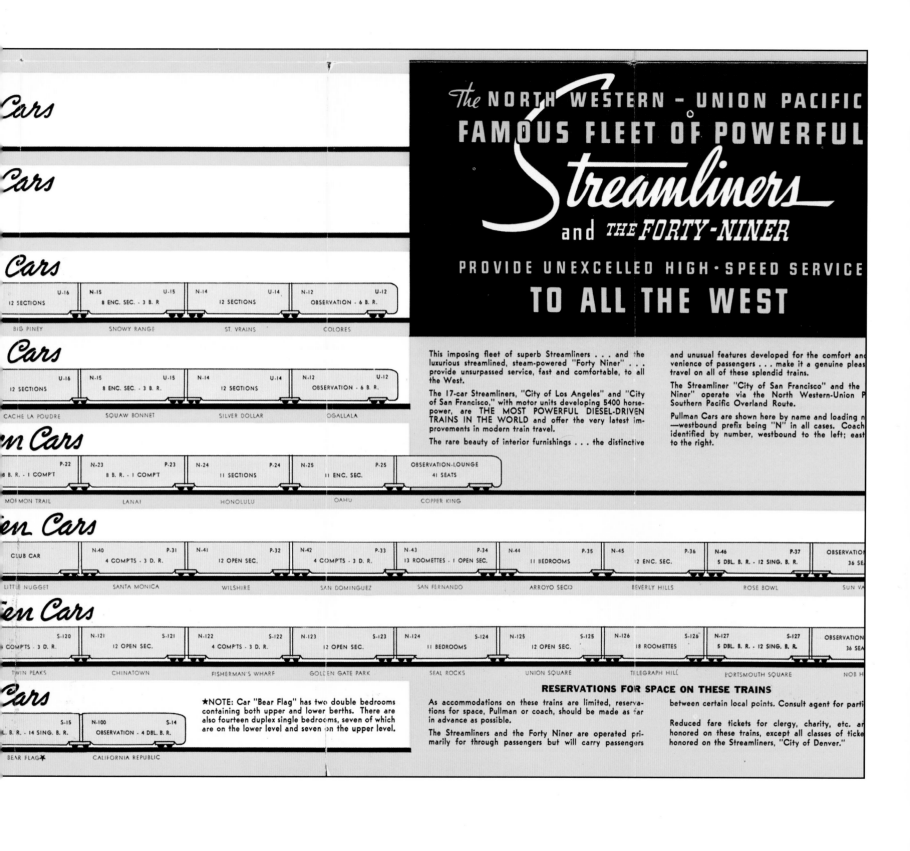

This imposing fleet of superb Streamliners . . . and the luxurious streamlined, steam-powered "Forty Niner" . . . provide unsurpassed service, fast and comfortable, to all the West.

The 17-car Streamliners, "City of Los Angeles" and "City of San Francisco," with motor units developing 5400 horsepower, are THE MOST POWERFUL DIESEL-DRIVEN TRAINS IN THE WORLD and offer the very latest improvements in modern train travel.

The rare beauty of interior furnishings . . . the distinctive and unusual features developed for the comfort and convenience of passengers . . . make it a genuine pleasure to travel on all of these splendid trains.

The Streamliner "City of San Francisco" and the Forty Niner" operate via the North Western-Union P[acific]-Southern Pacific Overland Route.

Pullman Cars are shown here by name and loading n[umber] —westbound prefix being "N" in all cases. Coach[es] identified by number, westbound to the left; eas[tbound] to the right.

Car diagrams (left-to-right):

U-16	N-15	U-15	N-14	U-14	N-12	U-12
12 SECTIONS	8 ENC. SEC. - 3 B.R.	12 SECTIONS			OBSERVATION - 6 B.R.	
BIG PINEY	SNOWY RANGE	ST. VRAINS			COLORES	

U-16	N-15	U-15	N-14	U-14	N-12	U-12
12 SECTIONS	8 ENC. SEC. - 3 B.R.	12 SECTIONS			OBSERVATION - 6 B.R.	
CACHE LA POUDRE	SQUAW BONNET	SILVER DOLLAR			OGALLALA	

8 B.R. - 1 COMP'T	P-22	N-23	P-23	N-24	P-24	N-25	P-25	OBSERVATION-LOUNGE
		8 B.R. - 1 COMP'T		11 SECTIONS		11 ENC. SEC.		41 SEATS
MORMON TRAIL	LANAI	HONOLULU		OAHU		COPPER KING		

N-40	P-31	N-41	P-32	N-42	P-33	N-43	P-34	N-44	P-35	N-45	P-36	N-46	P-37	OBSERVATION
CLUB CAR	4 COMPTS - 3 D.R.	12 OPEN SEC.	4 COMPTS - 3 D.R.		13 ROOMETTES - 1 OPEN SEC.		11 BEDROOMS		12 ENC. SEC.		5 DBL. B.R. - 12 SING. B.R.			36 SEATS
LITTLE NUGGET	SANTA MONICA	WILSHIRE	SAN DOMINGUEZ	SAN FERNANDO		ARROYO SECO		BEVERLY HILLS		ROSE BOWL		SUN VA...

4 COMPTS - 3 D.R.	S-120	N-121	S-121	N-122	S-122	N-123	S-123	N-124	S-124	N-125	S-125	N-126	S-126	N-127	S-127	OBSERVATION
	12 OPEN SEC.		4 COMPTS - 3 D.R.		12 OPEN SEC.		11 BEDROOMS		12 OPEN SEC.		18 ROOMETTES		5 DBL. B.R. - 12 SING. B.R.			36 SEATS
TWIN PEAKS	CHINATOWN	FISHERMAN'S WHARF		GOLDEN GATE PARK		SEAL ROCKS		UNION SQUARE		TELEGRAPH HILL		PORTSMOUTH SQUARE		NOB H...

B.R. - 14 SING. B.R.	S-15	N-100	S-14
		OBSERVATION - 4 DBL. B.R.	
BEAR FLAG★		CALIFORNIA REPUBLIC	

★NOTE: Car "Bear Flag" has two double bedrooms containing both upper and lower berths. There are also fourteen duplex single bedrooms, seven of which are on the lower level and seven on the upper level.

RESERVATIONS FOR SPACE ON THESE TRAINS

As accommodations on these trains are limited, reservations for space, Pullman or coach, should be made as far in advance as possible.

The Streamliners and the Forty Niner are operated primarily for through passengers but will carry passengers between certain local points. Consult agent for parti[culars].

Reduced fare tickets for clergy, charity, etc. ar[e] honored on these trains, except all classes of ticke[ts] honored on the Streamliners, "City of Denver."

UNION PACIFIC *STREAMLINER*
"CITY OF DENVER"

CITY OF LOS ANGELES
This swift, superbly appointed extra fare train, providing the finest to be had in luxurious travel comfort, carries both Pullmans and reserved seat coaches between Chicago and Los Angeles. Promotional copy

CITY OF SAN FRANCISCO
This sleek streamliner operates on a fast, daily schedule via NorthWestern-Union Pacific-Southern Pacific between Chicago and San Francisco. It is the "last word" in travel comfort, offering coach and all types of sleeping accommodations, dining cars and lounge cars. Promotional copy

Thus, on June 18, 1936 twin 10-car *City of Denver* trains behind A-B locomotive sets began daily service on the 1,048-mile route. The overnight 16-hour service averaged 65 mph, including eight stops. Travelers used to rattan coach seats or Pull-man plush were agape at the new finery.

A total of 182 patrons could be accommodated in their *City of Denver* assigned seats or berths. Lounge, diner or observation seats were considered non-revenue. The public areas of the train were painted in pastel colors, accented with aluminum. Linoleum or carpet contrasted with walls and seat colors in a harmonious blend.

That harmonious blend exploded into an Old West gunfight in the *City of Denver's Frontier Shack* lounge car. Decorated with plain pine boards for walls and horizontal poles "holding up" the wooden ceiling, it was an instant hit. "Wanted" posters of long-dead outlaws and replica six-shooters adorned the walls, and there was even a crying towel at the bar. Business boomed, sometimes filling the 32-seat lounge to standing room only. Apparently the yesteryear aura was just the ambiance needed by a Depression-weary public.

Additional cars and other motive power changes occurred in 1939 and 1940 on the *City of Denver*. Still, the train rolled on with a minimum of equipment changes for the decade from 1936 until post-war 1946 saw the floodgate of new equipment begin to open.

In 1936 the UP significantly raised the stakes in the corporate poker game with SP, Burlington and Santa Fe. Both the accountants and the traveling public were impressed with the results. Southern Pacific's contribution to the pre-war streamliners would be especially memorable.

THE MOST BEAUTIFUL TRAIN IN THE WORLD, SP'S *DAYLIGHT*

No railroad dominated California like the Southern Pacific. For several generations, when freight or passengers moved between California and Orgeon, New Mexico or Texas, the SP got a slice of the action. So, too, did SP feel the business collapse of the early 1930s.

Aware of the lightweight speedsters being built for neighbors UP and Burlington, the SP considered the same, but ultimately rejected the pocket streamliner. President Angus McDonald decreed that the new SP streamliner would be full-sized, fully appointed and first class—all hallmarks of the railroad he ran—and so it was.

Born in the massive erecting halls of Lima and Pullman-Standard came what would become known as "The Most Beautiful Train in the World." The first version's 12 cars stretched 870 feet from end to end, and two sets were required. Also, six new 5,000 hp GS-2 Class 4-8-4 locomotives powered the train. The total cost was more

"Daylight" Streamline Train
Southern Pacific Co.   SP 203

"The Most Beautiful Train in the World," is how Southern Pacific positioned its Daylight, *a 12-car streamlined train pulled by a semi-streamlined GS-2 4-8-4 steam locomotive.*

103

507—Southern Pacific "Daylight" Coast Line, Los Angeles to San Francisco, California

© CURT TEICH & CO., INC.   OB-H679

than $2 million in 1935 funds. "Yes, please!" said McDonald in perhaps the greatest gamble of his career.

Press releases built public interest throughout 1936 as the equipment took shape in Chicago and Lima, Ohio. Finally, in December, the engines left Lima under their own power. Semi-streamlined, with a red, orange and black paint scheme designed by Chester Mack, they were showstoppers. Stretching 108 feet, with drivers 73" in diameter and 250 lbs of boiler pressure, they showed off Lima in perhaps its finest hour. Designed to roll the 626-ton *Daylight* at 80 mph or climb a 2.2% grade without helpers, the engines met their specifications and more. SP's Chief Mechanical Officer Frank Russell called them "a sweet job," and his pride was well justified.

The *Daylight* consisted of several articulated two-unit coaches, plus a coffee shop/tavern lounge car. Parlor service was available, as well as a full diner and, of course, the lounge observation. All cars were air conditioned. The coaches had fully reclining seats, completely coordinated with the overall color scheme in each car. The "picture windows" were massive, over 5 feet wide and double glazed.

The dining car featured green walls and carpet, accented by rust colored upholstered aluminum framed chairs. It seated 40 and a wait was frequently necessary. The lounge car featured engraved glass panels and multi-colored neon lighting that "zinged" on the bar front. Chrome accents and venetian blinds offset the semi-circular seating in the tavern lounge. The cool, conservative parlor cars were decorated in green and tan, with wall-to-wall carpeting, drapes, venetian blinds and fully adjustable seats. It was a magnificent spot to unwind after a brief—or lengthy—visit to the lounge or diner.

Finally, on March 21, 1937 movie star Miss Olivia de Havilland swung a bottle of (presumably) California champagne against GS-2's #4411 pilot and officially christened SP Train 99, *The Daylight*. It left Los Angeles promptly at 8:15, as did its southbound counterpart at San Francisco. When the runs ended, 471 miles and 9 hours, 45 minutes later, the *Daylights* had carried the most passengers recorded on a single train set, and those travelers consumed a record amount of food and drink as well. In the process the *Daylights* showed the most profit per train mile on the SP system.

RIDE THE MOST BEAUTIFUL TRAIN IN AMERICA

See a hundred miles of Pacific Ocean on your Southern Pacific California trip!

THE TAVERN on the *Daylight* is lined with cozy leather booths and illuminated with soft, colored lights. In this congenial atmosphere, you'll spend happy hours while California's beautiful coastal scenery glides by.

FOUR SCENIC ROUTES TO CALIFORNIA

1 SHASTA ROUTE
2 OVERLAND ROUTE
3 GOLDEN STATE ROUTE
4 SUNSET ROUTE

WEST COAST OF MEXICO ROUTE

SOUTHERN PACIFIC S.S. LINES

63,060 passengers in three months, 143,851 in six months, 198,540 in nine months! That's the impressive record of Southern Pacific's new *Daylight*, the most beautiful train in America. Every day this brilliant streamlined train speeds between Los Angeles and San Francisco over the route of the California Missions, through rolling mountains and rich valleys, following the very edge of the Pacific Ocean for more than a hundred miles.

Whether your Pacific Coast destination is Los Angeles, San Francisco, Portland or Seattle, you can include this *Daylight* trip in your ticket by going west on *one* of Southern Pacific's Four Scenic Routes and returning on *another* SP route (see explanation at right).

Costing more than $2,000,000, custom-built from stem to stern, the twin *Daylights* are the "flagships" of an impressive fleet of brand new trains recently placed in service by Southern Pacific. In the year just past, the thrifty *Californian* and *San Francisco Challenger*, the royal *Forty-Niner*, the new *Cascade*, the *Sunbeam* in Texas and the giant new streamliner *City of San Francisco* joined the *Golden State Limited*, the *Overland Limited*, the *Sunset Limited* and the other famous trains that serve the Southern Pacific West.

HOW TO SEE TWICE AS MUCH ON YOUR TRIP WEST

The *Daylight* is just one bonus you enjoy on a Southern Pacific ticket to the Coast. We have Four Scenic Routes to California (see map). By going on one of these routes and returning on another one, you see a different part of the United States each way. You see *twice as much* of California and the West as you would by going and returning on the same route. You enjoy the *Daylight* ride between Los Angeles and San Francisco. And from most eastern and midwestern places, such a "go one way, return another" SP ticket costs you not one cent more rail fare than the usual back-and-forth round trip.

FREE TRAVEL SERVICE! For Southern Pacific's liberally illustrated travel guide, *How to See the Whole Pacific Coast*, write O. P. Bartlett, Dept. SE-3, 310 So. Michigan Avenue, Chicago. He will also send you a post card for you to mail if you wish a detailed routing, with costs. No charge for this service. No obligation.

Southern Pacific's representatives in principal eastern cities are authorities on the West. They will be glad to personally assist you plan your trip. See your telephone directory.

SOUTHERN PACIFIC

SOUTHERN PACIFIC LINES

THE WEST'S GREATEST TRANSPORTATION SYSTEM

105

FOREWORD

TO ALL STEWARDESS-NURSES:

The employment of your professional talents by this Company is in the nature of a precautionary measure which emanates from our unceasing quest of SAFETY - a word you will hear often as your railroad career progresses.

Your training has taught you to act quickly and think correctly. In your new environment you will have innumerable opportunities to apply your intelligence. The personality factor is most important in our business. You have contacted many people during your training; you will contact all manner of people enroute, but under differing conditions. Develop a genuine smile and a spirit of never-ending cheerfulness, and where sorrow is evident, you understand the value of deep sympathy.

The railroad is a public servant, but we cannot force the public to ride on our trains; we can only attract them through expensive advertising and active solicitation. When they favor us with their patronage they automatically become our guests and we must bend every effort to make them comfortable and happy. If we fail in this, we lose a friend, and when we lose a friend we lose a part of our only source of income. The management has high hopes for your application of gracious hospitality.

Make it a point to have a casual chat with the ladies. In this manner a quick reaction to our service can be obtained and correctives applied, if necessary.

Your training will make you particularly solicitous of the welfare of elderly people and children.

You will, by your actions, impress train crews with your desire to be cooperative. The conductors particularly are men of long and faithful service and their advice is generally sound.

Acquaint yourself with the time-table. Absorb the descriptive matter contained in our advertising. Get acquainted with the Passenger Agents at both terminals, also at the principal intermediate points, and call upon them for assistance where necessary.

You have been selected for the position of stewardess because of your thorough training, resourcefulness and general ability. Your conduct, both on and off duty, should always be such as to reflect the highest honor to the profession and your employers. You should cultivate a cheerful disposition, likewise a pleasing manner of speech and a friendly attitude at all times toward the general public and your fellow employes. Such action will create a favorable impression and a high regard for our services.

GENERAL INSTRUCTIONS TO STEWARDESS-NURSES.

1. At stations you are to be on platform at entrance of chair car for women and children, to direct passengers. You are not to handle baggage for patrons but when passenger is not utilizing service of redcap, inform them chair car porter will be glad to assist them.
2. At terminals and at intermediate stops, if the weather is uncomfortably cold or stormy, you may remain in the vestibule or inside the car but within call in event assistance is required.
3. You are not required to wear jackets while inside of trains nor on platforms at intermediate stations during hot weather. Caps will be worn on platform, in diners, and on trips through the train. They may be removed at other times.
4. You will not assist porter or brakemen in loading or unloading hand baggage, but will render obvious assistance to elderly persons, those with infirmities as well as women with small children
5. Women's coaches are for the exclusive use of women and children; boys over seven years of age are not permitted in the car; boys under seven who are large for their age must be required to use lavatory facilities other than those contained in the lounge room. In carrying out these provisions, if any difficulty is encountered, report matter to Train Conductor at once.
6. Trainmen and porter will when practicable make arrangements with you before entering women's car and in your company.
7. Men may escort female members of their families into women's coaches at terminals with your permission and in your company.
8. At the commencement of each conductor's run, while you are on duty, arrange at convenience of the conductor to accompany him through the train and open for him the facilities set aside for women in each car.
9. Inspections of entire train, observing temperature, ventilation, cleanliness of women's toilets, car floors, etc., are to be made six times a day - twice in the morning, twice in the afternoon and twice in the evening. If temperature is not comfortable due to improper operation of air-conditioning equipment, call this condition to the attention of the porter or Conductor so he may make proper adjustment.
10. Coach lights will be dimmed by member of train crew at 10 P.M.
11. In the event of complaint of heat or cold in a coach, it is often possible to satisfy and increase the comfort of the passenger by moving him or her to a different location in the car.
12. Under ordinary circumstances, each passenger is supplied with one pillow. However, if situation develops where additional pillows are desired, there is no objection to providing them.
13. Proper functioning of air-conditioning units requires that doors of air-conditioned cars should be kept closed.
14. In case of personal injury, assist the conductor in ascertaining name, destination and other pertinent facts in connection with the injury. In such cases your professional training may be valuable in ascertaining the extent of the injury.
15. If passengers become ill or injured on train, render first aid at once, consulting conductor if case seems to warrant further attention. In case coach passenger becomes seriously ill and must lie down, arrange with Pullman conductor for berth in tourist car for this purpose without charge to the passenger.
16. Your services are for the entire passenger list and under no circumstances are you to function exclusively for any one passenger or group. You will under no circumstances undertake to attend intoxicated persons unless their intemperance has made them ill and they require medical attention. All other cases should be referred to the attention of the conductor.
17. Do not call for a doctor against the wishes of a passenger unless in your professional opinion the case warrants such action. Contact conductor who will telegraph ahead for a company surgeon to meet the train. A list of company surgeons and their locations is shown in Employe's working time tables. Familiarize yourself with this list and also the location of hospitals.
18. If it is necessary to handle a passenger in wheel chair, advance arrangements must be made through the conductor. Such passenger will be taken off car after other passengers have been unloaded and you will see that the passenger so handled is made as comfortable as is possible.
19. Following is rule covering transportation of persons infected with infectious, contagious or loathesome diseases as contained in Circular No. 3698 issued by Southern Pacific Railway Company June 10, 1933:
   "(a) When permitted by health authorities to travel, all persons afflicted with diseases the nature of which, in the carriers' judgment and in the interest of other passengers, would require isolation insofar as it is possible to isolate such persons, will, if not traveling in special car for their own use, be required to purchase room space for themselves and for any and all attendants who may be accompanying them."
   Representatives arranging for movements of any passengers of this type will follow the rule quoted. Should, however, any passengers be offered for movement on the Californian or become so infected enroute which to your judgment comes under this ruling, please call attention immediately to Train Conductor so action can be taken to protect all other passengers in the train.
20. Hours of service on trains are 6:30 AM to 10:30 PM. You are subject to call during the night.
21. First Aid Kit will be provided by Chief Surgeon and must be available at all times on the train.
22. While we do not encourage the transportation of children unaccompanied by parent or guardian, you will have some cases of this kind. When children are traveling alone, the name and address of the person sending them should be obtained whenever possible, and after arrival at destination (when at a station on the RI-SP) a telegram over your signature and title as "Stewardess-Nurse" should be forwarded to the General Passenger Agent at Chicago, Kansas City, El Paso, Phoenix, or Los Angeles, or representative arranging the trip, advising of their safe arrival. Telegrams should be sent over company wires and read somewhat as follows:
   "_____ safely arrived _____
   (child's name)   (destination)
   today after a pleasant trip. Notify parents or guardians."
   adding any other pertinent information that you may desire. Money given to you for expenditure in child's behalf shall be accounted for on form provided for this purpose.
23. You should always bear in mind that the executive authority aboard a train is vested in the conductor.
24. Your position precludes your accepting gratuities of whatsoever nature; you will not accept meal invitations from passengers. Develop an effective and yet appropriate declination.
25. Your meals enroute will be obtained in the diner for which you will sign checks. Meals should not taken at a time when the dining car facilities are required to take care of passengers.
26. During periods of heavy travel, if the diner becomes congested, arrange to confer with the Steward and render such assistance to passengers as may in your judgment be appropriate.
27. There is a change of time at Tucumcari and Yuma. Do not fail to change your watch before departing from these points.
28. You are prohibited from exchanging hand signals with members of crews of passing trains.
29. In the course of your trip if you observe any part of the service which can be modified or corrected to add to the comfort or convenience of passengers, report at end of trip to General Passenger Agent.
30. Uniforms should be worn only while on duty or enroute to or from the train. Your attire must be perfect at all times. During your training, your appearance had meticulous attention. We expect no less vigilance on the Golden State Route.

—From Manual for Stewardesses, Rock Island Lines—Southern Pacific System, March 1, 1937.

Dick Bowers

Southern Pacific's Lark *slips through Santa Susana Pass enroute to her Los Angeles destination.*

By June the *Daylights* had handled 88,830 passengers between Los Angeles and San Francisco, but had to turn thousands away. Over a quarter of a million passengers rode the service its first year alone. More equipment was the answer, and it was promptly designed and ordered.

On January 2, 1940 the all-new, 14-car *Daylight* was placed in service. These cars included an ingenious baggage elevator system which lifted passenger's bags directly into the car alongside the vestibule. It saved strain and made boarding a snap.

More articulated coaches were in this super *Daylight*, but the *piece-de-resistance* was its triple-articulated coffee shop-kitchen-dining car. Stretching over 203 feet, with the kitchen articulated in the center, it fed 152 simultaneously, and lunch was only $1.50. Other articulated cars became a hallmark of post-war SP passenger service on the *Lark, Cascade, Shasta Daylight* and others.

Beautifully appointed parlor-lounge-observa-

L-1   La Grange, Illinois, Home of the Streamline

OB-H465

EMC in La Grange, Illinois, wanting to participate in the new era of streamlined passenger trains, billed itself as Home of the Streamline(r). On December 31, 1930, General Motors bought the Electro-Motive Company (EMC), and subsequently became a leading player in the diesel train market.

tions marked the rear of the *Daylight*, and even more powerful GS-4 engines provided the muscle. Indeed, these engines became a symbol of the SP to such an extent, that one, #4449, ultimately was restored to become the power for the 1975-77 American Freedom Train. Any who saw it, even half a continent away from SP property, admired the power, beauty and grace Lima, Chester Mack and SP embodied in these engines. A *Daylight* was worthy to handle our National Heritage.

With the new equipment in service, the original 1937 *Daylights* were given a quick reconditioning, and on March 30, 1940 were back in business as the *Noon Daylights*. Success bred more success, and by year's end another 20 engines and 30 passenger cars were on order for more and longer *Daylights* and other services. Both engines and cars were put to good use.

On May 1, 1941 the overnight *Lark* on the San Francisco-Los Angeles route was streamlined and powered by one of the new *Daylight* Class 4-8-4 locomotives. By year's end more and more of SP's regular passenger trains went behind the new engines, as WWII descended. As the coastal carri-

er from Portland to New Orleans, the SP moved freight and passengers like never before or since.

MILE-HIGH MODERNISM:

The streamliner momentum which had started with the *Pioneer Zephyr* was not to abate until forcibly halted by WWII. As fast as new Burlington *Zephyrs* were delivered, they were filled with paying passengers.

In the spring of 1936 the Burlington knew that within days the UP would begin *City of Denver* service. Unfortunately, the abuilding luxurious *Denver Zephyr* was still several months away from completion at Budd and EMC.

With a stroke of genius, and to minimize the new *City* competition, on June 1, 1936 Ralph Budd inaugurated the *Advance Denver Zephyrs*, really the *Pioneer Zephyr* and sister #9903. They got the first press—18 days before the *City* service began—and protected the Q's mail contract.

Finally, on October 23, 1936 the first *Denver Zephyr* set out from Chicago for Denver. Another go-for-broke publicity speed run, it was called the "Gentlemen's Adventure," and completely sanctioned by the Burlington. The 1,017 mile trip took 12 hours, 12 minutes and averaged 83.3

EMD

Chris Burritt

Newly-built General Pershing Zephyr, *the #9908 Model AA, takes a test spin at EMC's La Grange, Illinois facilities. It was built by Budd and powered by EMC in April, 1939. The locomotive pulled the St. Louis to Kansas City Burlington train, averaging 55.8 mph. It could haul three cars and was the last of the "shovel noses."*

Inset: Sitting in the Burlington roundhouse at Galesburg, Illinois in 1964, the Silver Charger awaits its destiny. The unit later was shipped to the Museum of Transport in St. Louis for future generations to inspect.

Budd

A ceremony to mark the inaugural of the General Pershing Zephyr ensues in 1939. A bottle of champagne hangs suspended above the speaker's platform to break against the locomotive's pilot.

PIONEER ZEPHYR
Completely Air-Conditioned
No Extra Fare

NORTHBOUND—No. 21	SOUTHBOUND—No. 20
Solarium-Parlor Lounge	**Solarium-Parlor-Lounge**
Kansas City to Omaha-Lincoln	Lincoln-Omaha to Kansas City
Coaches—Kansas City to Omaha-Lincoln	**Coaches**—Lincoln-Omaha to Kansas City
Buffet-Grill Service—For all meals	**Buffet-Grill Service**—For all meals
NORTHBOUND—No. 23	**SOUTHBOUND—No. 22**
Sleeping Cars A C	**Sleeping Cars A C**
Kansas City to Omaha—D.R., Sections	Lincoln and Omaha to Kansas City—
(May be occupied until 8.00 a.m.)	D.R., Sections (Ready at Lincoln and
Kansas City to Lincoln via Omaha—	Omaha 9.30 p.m.)
D.R., Sections (Ready at Kansas City	**Chair Car A C**
10.00 p.m.)	Omaha to Kansas City
Chair Car A C—Kansas City to Omaha	**Coach**
and Lincoln	Lincoln to Omaha
NORTHBOUND—No. 27	**SOUTHBOUND—No. 26**
Dining-Parlor Car A C	**Dining-Parlor Car A C**
Kansas City to Omaha	Omaha to Kansas City
Coach A C—Kansas City to Omaha	**Coach A C**—Omaha to Kansas City

-1937
Burlington
Timetable

EMD

A 10-car Zephyr *streamliner,
headed by the* Silver King,
*whisks down the prairie rails
between Denver and Chicago.
The 3,000 hp units were
given 16 hour schedules,
necessitating an average
speed of 65 miles an hour,
nine hours less than previous
schedules. The trains featured
chair cars with reclining
seats, sleeping cars, club car,
diner and rounded end
observation car.*

In June of 1936 the Advance Zephyrs *were initiated, carrying passengers the 1,034 miles between Chicago and Denver in comfort, convenience and economy. Free pillows, low cost meals, hostess, and radio were some of the highlights.*

mph, a long distance record which stood for years.

Two weeks later, on November 8, 1936 Jane Garlow, the granddaughter of Buffalo Bill Cody, rode her pinto pony up to the train's silver nose and christened it with a bottle of champagne. The 16-hour overnight service was under way. Service has continued until today, although under Amtrak since 1971 a slower schedule has prevailed.

Behind the two stainless steel-clad locomotives was a baggage-mail car, a baggage-dormitory-lounge car, two coaches, diner, four sleepers and a parlor-observation. All but the baggage-RPO,

lounge and observation were articulated sets. The locomotive was 3,000 hp, and should it fail, the Burlington had two massive 4-6-4 locomotives standing by. They were even shrouded in stainless steel supplied by Budd and appropriately named *Aeolus*, "Keeper of the Winds." Rarely were they needed.

New features included tightlock couplers, electro-pneumatic brakes and even extra-long berths. First class accommodations totaled 93 berths and 10 parlor seats; 102 could ride coach.

Once again decorated with the help of industrial designer Paul Cret, the *Denver Zephyr* made extensive use of fine woods in veneer form. New features included the first 110 volt outlets for that latest appliance, the electric razor. Fabrics such as rayon and nylon were used and the coach seats were covered in leather. Amenities included both a radio-phonograph and soda fountain in the lounge-observation. The dining car seated 40 in the usual splendor of drapes, venetian blinds, indirect lighting and air conditioning.

Interior design included carpeting, seat fabrics, walls, bulkheads and ceilings, all coordinated in a variety of pastel colors and stainless steel trim. Indeed, Paul Cret felt the 1936 *Denver Zephyr* was his finest creation. Perhaps it was. One awestruck observer commented, "He (Cret) can shake them out of his sleeve!" Certainly the crowds filled the train night after night.

Turning back to their continuing skirmish in the Twin Cities market, only seven weeks after introducing the *Denver Zephyr*, all-new 7-car articulated *Twin Zephyrs* were placed in that service. With all cars named after mythological beings, the trains soon became known as *"The Trains of the Gods and Goddesses."* The parlor-observations were named *Juno* and *Jupiter* while the locomotives were *Pegasus* and *Zephyrus*. Reading the car names was a classics lesson in itself.

The 7-car streamliners held 160 passengers in luxury, be it in coach or parlor car seats. Business was so good that in less than a year an eighth car was added to each equipment set. In 1940 timing on the *Morning Zephyr* was cut to a flat six hours between St. Paul and Chicago. The next new addition to the *Zephyr* fleet would have to wait until war's end.

OVERNIGHT · EVERYNIGHT

Burlington's **DENVER ZEPHYR**

BETWEEN CHICAGO AND DENVER

The names of the cars on the Denver Zephyr each began with the word "Silver" because of the train's gleaming exterior and also in honor of Colorado, the Silver State.

The spacious women's dressing room is bright and dainty with its robin's egg blue wash basins, cream colored leather chairs and sofa, and mirror extending almost the full width of the compartment. Two dressing rooms afford ample toilet facilities for men passengers.

The second coach, in which green and complementary shades are blended in delightful effect, seats 64 passengers in chairs that are adjustable to three semi-reclining positions and, likewise, can be turned to face the broad windows. Each chair in this coach has an individual ashtray.

The forward coach is softly colored in shades of blue, rust and cream. In addition to seats for 48 passengers, it contains an attractive dinette with seating capacity for 16 passengers.

Food service on board the Denver Zephyr was to be something remembered and savored by patrons. As the saying went, mealtimes on the Zephyr are Feast-ive Occasions.

113

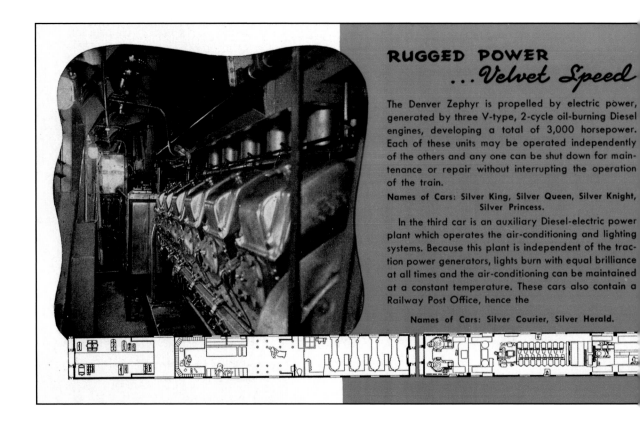

RUGGED POWER
...Velvet Speed

The Denver Zephyr is propelled by electric power, generated by three V-type, 2-cycle oil-burning Diesel engines, developing a total of 3,000 horsepower. Each of these units may be operated independently of the others and any one can be shut down for maintenance or repair without interrupting the operation of the train.

Names of Cars: Silver King, Silver Queen, Silver Knight, Silver Princess.

In the third car is an auxiliary Diesel-electric power plant which operates the air-conditioning and lighting systems. Because this plant is independent of the traction power generators, lights burn with equal brilliance at all times and the air-conditioning can be maintained at a constant temperature. These cars also contain a Railway Post Office, hence the

Names of Cars: Silver Courier, Silver Herald.

The Denver Zephyr at Galesburg, Illinois shows the streamliner next to a water column, used to water steam locomotives. The new streamliners eventually would replace steam power on all railroads.

Famous "Denver Zephyr" and C.B.&Q.R.R. Station, Galesburg, Ill.

114

The Denver Zephyr *covered the 1,000-plus miles between Chicago and Denver in about 16½ hours in 1950.*

The Denver Zephyr
OVERNIGHT, EVERYNIGHT, BETWEEN CHICAGO AND DENVER

The Denver Zephyrs run between Chicago and Denver in just overnight. Westbound they span 1,034 miles in 16 hours, 30 minutes; eastbound 1,039 miles in 16 hours, 5 minutes. The Denver Zephyrs have achieved one of the most amazing on-time performance records in railroad history.

A. COTSWORTH, JR., *Passenger Traffic Manager*
547 W. Jackson Blvd., Chicago, Ill.

W. M. MOLONEY, *General Agent, Passenger Dept.*
101 W. Adams (at Clark) St., Chicago, Ill.

F. W. JOHNSON, *General Passenger Agent*
17th & Champa St., Denver, Colo.

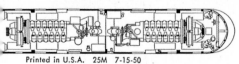

Printed in U.S.A. 25M 7-15-50

DAILY SCHEDULE—Corrected to July 1, 1950

Westbound—Read Down			Eastbound—Read Up	
5:00 PM	Lv.	Chicago (CST)	Ar.	9:05 AM
		Aurora	Ar.	M 8:25 AM
7:09 PM	Lv.	Galesburg	Ar.	6:46 AM
7:51 PM	Lv.	Burlington	Ar.	6:03 AM
8:58 PM	Lv.	Ottumwa	Ar.	4:51 AM
10:44 PM	Lv.	Creston	Ar.	3:05 AM
A12:08 AM	Ar.	Council Bluffs		
12:30 AM	Ar.	Omaha	Lv.	1:15 AM
1:45 AM	Ar.	Lincoln	Lv.	12:11 AM
3:23 AM	Ar.	Hastings	Lv.	10:41 PM
	Ar.	Minden	Lv.	D 10:08 PM
S 4:12 AM	Ar.	Holdrege	Lv.	9:49 PM
		Oxford	Lv.	9:24 PM
5:32 AM	Ar.	McCook (CST)	Lv.	8:38 PM
6:40 AM	Ar.	Akron (MT)	Lv.	5:39 PM
7:13 AM	Ar.	Fort Morgan	Lv.	C 5:07 PM
8:30 AM	Ar.	Denver (MT)	Lv.	4:00 PM

A—Stops to let off revenue passengers from Chicago.
C—Stops to receive revenue passengers for Lincoln and east when notified at Denver.
D—Stop to let off revenue passengers from Denver or to receive revenue passengers for Lincoln and east when notified at Holdrege.
M—Stops to let off revenue passengers from Denver.
S—Stops to let off revenue passengers from Burlington or beyond and to receive revenue passengers for Denver.

Chris Burritt

◄► Whoof went Burlington's "Mark Twain" Zephyr across Nebraska recently when it set a new world's record of 122 miles per hour. Engineer Jack Ford (inset) was at the controls. Photo is personally signed and dated by engineer Jack Ford.

In 1937 the Burlington needed stand-by protection for its Zephyrs, but it needed something stylish, so it took this S-4 4-6-4 and draped the conventional steam locomotive with a stainless steel shroud that resembles Zephyr styling. Aeolus (Keeper of the Winds) also had a streamlined sister, #4001.

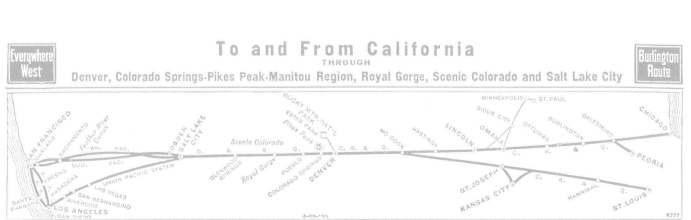

To and From California
THROUGH
Denver, Colorado Springs-Pikes Peak-Manitou Region, Royal Gorge, Scenic Colorado and Salt Lake City

Everywhere West

Burlington Route

Still new and still in the erecting bays, Silver King *is visited by the curious.*

C&NW'S CHALLENGE: THE '400s'

The true instigator of the great speed war between the Twin Cities and Chicago was the last to field streamlined equipment. On January 2, 1935 the Chicago & North Western had started steam powered service with regular cars. Of course, the *Hiawatha* and *Zephyr* competition was not long in coming. However, it took nearly five years before the first "400" was streamlined. Two 10-car sets from Pullman-Standard with twin Electro-Motive locomotives were ordered, constructed and delivered in the space of eight months. Each set stretched 960 feet, weighed 885 tons and seated 486 passengers.

Matching the 6 1/2 hour schedule of its competitors, the green and yellow streamliner joined the fray on September 24, 1939. Accommodations included coach, parlor car and full lounge and dining service.

Coaches featured reclining seats, while the parlors looked like nothing more than a "La-Z-boy" saleman's dream! The lounge seats were upholstered in red leather, which reflected off the glass and aluminum trim throughout. The diner was stocked with all the comforts of home. Its decor included green leather chairs, pink and dark red

THE NEW STREAMLINER "400" — CHICAGO AND NORTH WESTERN LINE

NORTH WESTERN'S NEW "400" STREAMLINER OPERATING DAILY BETWEEN CHICAGO AND ST. PAUL-MINNEAPOLIS VIA MILWAUKEE

Jay Christopher

Dressed out in bright yellow and green, and a colorful insignia on the nose to boot, the C&NW 400 trains were hot competition for the Milwaukee's Hiawathas *and the Burlington's* Zephyrs.

Cars 7200-7201 were built for use on the Twin Cities 400 *trains, having been manufactured by the Pullman-Standard Car Mfg. Co. in Chicago in 1939. The parlor-solarium cars had 12 parlor seats, 20 lounge seats and nine solarium seats.*

THE FAMOUS "400" STREAMLINER FLEET — CHICAGO AND NORTH WESTERN LINE

ULTRA-MODERN PARLOR CARS ON THE "400" FLEET

Jay Christopher

The 400 streamliner trains featured aesthetically pleasing colors, fabrics and patterns. Murals such as seen at the ends of the cars added interest, and even special lighting effects were considered.

THE FAMOUS "400" STREAMLINER FLEET — CHICAGO AND NORTH WESTERN LINE

THE TWIN CITIES "400" OBSERVATION LOUNGE CAR — SPEEDOMETER IN CAR SHOWN IN INSERT

In this observation car, a speedometer is located at the rear of the car to give travelers the latest readings. A bench chair was situated at the rear so passengers could relax while they viewed the passing scenery.

carpeting, matching drapes and plenty of waiters. The parlor-observation interior was blue and apricot. Passengers gazed out venetian blind-equipped windows and watched the scenery unwind while the speedometer hovered near 100.

Business boomed. By early in WWII the C&NW had enough equipment in place to partially re-equip the 1939 "*400*" and field a whole "*400*" fleet running across its Illinois, Wisconsin, Minnesota and upper Michigan territory. None lasted until Amtrak.

"The 400" reads the inscription on the rear observation car of the train. That alone said fast service in luxury accommodations.

The Chicago & NorthWestern coach yards are teeming with all manner of early streamliner trains. One of the earliest trains is located right behind the wash rack in the center of the yard.

125

THE ROCK ISLAND LINE IS
A MIGHTY FINE ROAD

As the fabled carrier of song and legend, the Chicago, Rock Island & Pacific in its day was a "Mighty Fine Road." Also beset with the Depression era traffic losses its stronger rivals Burlington and UP suffered, the "Rock" responded in like manner.

Once having secured the blessing of its bankruptcy trustee, in 1936 the RI retained Budd to build six short coach streamliners and Electro-Motive to power them. The equipment arrived in 1937, gleaming stainless steel, behind a red, maroon and silver locomotive paint scheme straight out of EMC's design section. Even the locomotives were unique, since their combination of a single, 1,200 hp V-16 and two, twin-axle, all-powered trucks had not been seen before in the industry. Ultimately, the design resurfaced in 1939 as the basis for the Electro-Motive FT freight diesel, which spelled the end of the steam locomotive.

Truly, when the new *Rockets* flashed through the sleepy granger towns of the Midwest, people stopped. For example, the consist of the 1937 *Des Moines Rocket* between its namesake city and Chicago was typical: a single streamlined locomotive, baggage-dinette car, two coaches and a parlor-observation. Similar service was also provided by the *Peoria Rocket* in 1937, and by 1940 the *Choctaw Rocket* serviced Memphis-Amarillo and the *Texas Rocket* covered Kansas City to Dallas.

During October, 1937 one of these short coach-only sets was assigned to Denver-Kansas City service, but were no match for the Q and UP services. Returning November 12, 1939 the RI installed the *Rocky Mountain Rocket* in the best Electro-Motive and Pullman-Standard streamliner tradition.

The two 7-car sets had 19 1/2 hour schedules and contained reclining seat coaches, a diner-lounge and full sleeping car services including a sleeper-lounge-observation. Interior design was a match for the competition, including full carpet-

"The Mighty Fine Road," the Rock Island, which ran primarily between Chicago and San Francisco ordered six short-coach streamliners in 1937. The railroad operated 8,000 miles of track in 14 states.

TIME FLIES WITH THE ROCKETS

Budd

The Rock Island's beautiful colors of red, maroon and silver were very striking.

THE PEORIA-CHICAGO STREAMLINED ROCKET

ing, wide windows and various coordinated paint schemes of tan, pearl and grey linking the entire train set. The 25-seat lounge-observation featured Flexwood on its walls and a built-in radio. The diner-lounge seated 32 for dinner and 14 in the cocktail section.

The *Rocky Mountain Rocket* split at Limon, Colorado with the main train going to Denver, and a shorter section headed for Colorado Springs. Between this service, and the brief joint operation of the *Arizona Limited* with the SP during the 1940-41 and 1941-42 winter seasons, the RI entered the annals of the streamliner saga with class and accomplishment.

Built in 1979 by EMC, this Rock Island Model TA stops with its train at Englewood Station in Chicago.

This 1,200-hp Rock Island #602 diesel is stopped at Des Moines, Iowa. The skirts below the frame help to make the unit more streamlined.

See how streamlined service steps up the tempo of travel! Only a few days ago the rail trip from Memphis, Tennessee, to Amarillo, Texas, and return, consumed 44 full hours. Now, thanks to the new *Choctaw Rocket*, that running time has been safely cut by 10 hours and 40 minutes . . . more than 24%!

The Choctaw Rocket, *train #52, ran from Memphis, Tennessee to Amarillo, Texas in about 33 hours roundtrip.*

Here's one of Rock Island's New Streamliners
CHOCTAW ROCKET
BUILT BY PULLMAN-STANDARD
THE WORLD'S LARGEST BUILDERS OF RAILROAD AND TRANSIT EQUIPMENT

The Diner—The hours one spends on the new streamliners pass as quickly as the miles. For radio, scenery and interesting travel companions provide diversions while the food has earned these *Rockets* an enviable reputation.

The Chair Car offers unusually wide shatterproof windows, improved air-conditioning, insulated silence, scientific lighting, chairs with contours that invite you to relax, soft of upholstery and adjustable to your complete comfort.

WITH the commissioning of the *Choctaw Rocket* by the Rock Island Lines—an ultra-modern train offering complete travel service—the most encouraging fact in the progress toward making streamlining everywhere available has been reaffirmed. It is, to paraphrase a familiar saw, that one good train deserves another!

For since the occasion on which Pullman-Standard introduced streamlining to America and set the standards of strength, safety and comfort by which all construction of this type is measured, every subsequent train has, through its popularity, extended rather than satisfied the ever-growing demand for this modern transportation.

Fundamentally, that is why The Rock Island has been able to expand its fleet to include this new streamliner, and also why its construction was entrusted to Pullman-Standard. Because of the overwhelming preference which you, the traveling public, have displayed for these new trains, the railroads have purchased over 70%* of their new lightweight equipment from Pullman-Standard.

*When this advertisement was written

In addition to railroad passenger cars, Pullman-Standard designs and manufactures freight, subway, elevated and street cars, trackless trolleys, air-conditioning systems, chilled tread car wheels and a complete line of car repair parts.

PULLMAN-STANDARD CAR MANUFACTURING CO.—CHICAGO
Copyright 1941, by Pullman-Standard Car Manufacturing Company

Pullman Accommodations: The double bedroom offers conveniences comparable to your own home. Two full-length beds, a full-length mirror, complete toilet facilities, a hinged table, individual controls for heat, light and ventilation, and plenty of storage space for clothes and luggage. Also available—economical single occupancy sections—lower and upper berths.

"Tops" IN STREAMLINERS ARE BUILT BY *Pullman-Standard*

Dick Bowers

New from EMC, this 1937 Texas Rocket *TA(meaning twelve hundred horse power A unit)*, was a good match for the three- or four-car stainless steel Budd passenger cars that accompanied it. The top rear corners of the unit (out of picture) tapered to meet the roof line of the matching cars. The bottom door in the nose housed a retractable coupler and the sloping front made the locomotive look sleek.

ROCKY MOUNTAIN ROCKET
At the Foot of Famous Pikes Peak

EMC-built E3A was the first mass-produced diesel passenger unit. Rock Island purchased two of these units (#625, #626) which were delivered in 1939; both were powered by two 12-567 prime movers and equipped with gearing required to go 110 mph. In these similar promotional views, the locomotive hauls the Rocky Mountain Rocket *between Chicago and Denver-Colorado Springs. The views were retouched in the railroad's darkroom, as the photo was actually taken in the Midwest and the mountains added later.*

EMD

GM-EMC 1939-built #7000
was a 2,000-hp E3A, developing 54,100 pounds of tractive
effort. The Eagle had landed.

'THE EAGLE HAS LANDED,'
MISSOURI PACIFIC STYLE

Another Midwest customer for a customized daytime coach-parlor streamliner was the Missouri Pacific. Contracting with American Car and Foundry to build a 6-car aluminum set, Raymond Loewy was also retained for styling and design. Thus was born the first of the famous blue and cream *Eagle* streamliners.

With its debut on March 10, 1940 the 6-car streamliner was coordinated from eagle wings on the EMC E-3 locomotive's nose to a similar pair under the rear-facing observation windows. Equipment included coaches, diner-lounge and parlor-observation. Once again Loewy's palette of pastel colors, aluminum trim, contrasting carpeting and overstuffed reclining seats worked their passenger magic. Business was brisk between St. Louis, Kansas City and Omaha that early spring morning. So brisk, that by October, 1942 the MP reported that the entire $1.1 million the two train sets had cost had been earned back from net income received.

With such an enthusiastic response, in 1941 the MP ordered two, 7-car coach-and-Pullman sets for

The Missouri Pacific's famous blue and cream Eagle streamliners were a big hit when they debuted in March of 1940. Even builder EMD was proud to proclaim the train's spectacular exterior appearance and interior comforts.

133

Even the Missouri Pacific timetables were colorful; this photo from a MP timetable shows diesel #7000 which the road was very proud of.

Missouri Pacific steak dinner card was used to promote the delicious foods served aboard the Eagle *streamlined trains.*

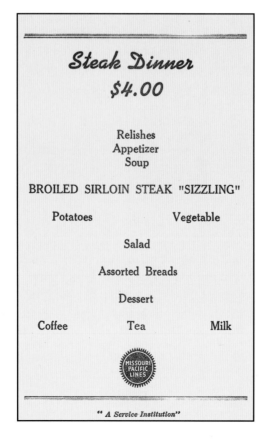

Steak Dinner
$4.00

Relishes
Appetizer
Soup

BROILED SIRLOIN STEAK "SIZZLING"

Potatoes   Vegetable

Salad

Assorted Breads

Dessert

Coffee   Tea   Milk

MISSOURI
PACIFIC
LINES

" A Service Institution"

service between St. Louis and Denver. To be operated in conjunction with the Denver & Rio Grande, the equipment was nearing completion on Pearl Harbor Day. After the shock of entering the war subsided somewhat, and War Production Board authority was granted, the streamliner quietly entered service on June 22, 1942, really a war baby, rather than the last of the pre-war coach-and-Pullman streamliners.

THE GREAT STEEL FLEET: NYC's *MERCURY, CENTURY* AND SISTERS

The New York Central System was extremely hard hit by the Depression. Over half its motive power and rolling stock had been sidelined. Thus, when it began to notice the public acceptance and profitability of the new Western streamliners, it decided to start slowly and in house.

In early 1935 the NYC retained famed industrial designer Henry Dreyfuss to design and coordinate the interior decor for the Central's first streamliner, the *Mercury.* Composed of rebuilt commuter coaches and a couple of sidelined 4-6-2 Pacifics, the initial train was nine cars long. What it lacked in length, it made up in style.

The locomotives were shrouded, bathtub style,

Noted industrial designer Henry Dreyfuss streamlined these 4,700-hp New York Central Hudson steam locomotives, built by the American Locomotive Company. The design conformed to the streamlined 20th Century Limited passenger train.

135

Pulsing with steam, the NYC streamlined Hudson's solid drivers exude strength and dependability.

Grand Central Terminal in New York City covered nearly 70 acres facing East 42nd Street, from Vanderbilt to Lexington Ave., the largest and most costly railroad station in the world at the time. The station had 31 miles of track under cover, with a capacity for handling 200 trains and 70,000 passengers per hour. There were 42 tracks for long distance express trains on the 42nd Street level and 25 tracks for suburban trains in the concourse.

Grand Central Terminal Station, New York City.

in a typical railroad so-so attempt at streamlining. However, new disk drivers were installed and floodlit at night. With the flashing chrome-vanadium driving rods reciprocating in that glare, the *Mercury* cut a striking image.

If the engine styling was lackluster, the gutted and rebuilt coaches were the "Train of Tomorrow." The public relations brochures proclaimed that the new *Mercury* should be thought of as a private club on wheels, and for good reason.

The new streamlined 20th Century Limited *during a run on the New York Central's main line tracks along the Hudson River.*

The train consisted of a combine, three coaches, a coach-kitchen car, a full dining car, a buffet-lounge car, a parlor and the parlor-observation. All cars were air-conditioned and had tight-lock couplers. The coaches contained adjustable seats, and coach passengers had their own smoking lounge in a portion of the coach-combine car.

New special dining car china and crystal were even designed for *Mercury* service. The dining car was rather unique in that Dreyfuss designed it in three sections or rooms. The adjacent lounge car was noted for a half-circle bar and plenty of NYC monogramed glassware. The bulkheads in both lounge and diner had large murals affixed. Dreyfuss even made each car's vestibules into circular entryways.

Smart style continued into the parlor-lounge-observation. Carpeted floor and the wide, unusual

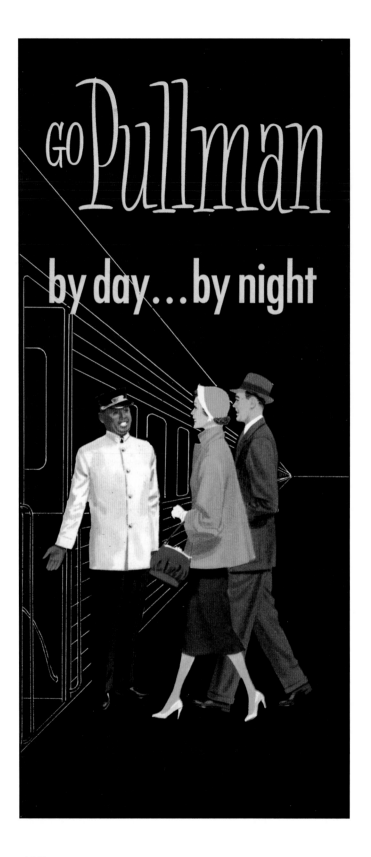

floor-to-ceiling glass solarium made it a very popular spot. The speedometer also drew rather regular attention.

Finally, on July 15, 1936 the first *Mercury* sped
on its way between Cleveland and Detroit. An
instant success, the NYC drew more commuter
coaches from storage, and on November 12, 1939
Chicago service via the *Mercury* joined the NYC
family. It was a near duplicate of the 1936 train,
but was hauled by a streamlined 4-6-4 Hudson
and had several more coaches in each consist.
Both trains continued to serve through the end of
WWII.

With his *Mercury* commission a resounding
success, Henry Dreyfuss was given the ultimate
NYC challenge: streamline its flagship, the *20th
Century Limited*.

Working with Alco in Schenectady, Dreyfuss
designed a bullet-nosed Hudson that looked
speedy, even at rest, and the NYC purchased 10.
They handled the *Century*, *Commodore Vanderbilt* and others

Pullman-Standard received a purchase order for
62 cars of various configurations to fully equip
four *Century* sets. It was promoted as the first all-
room train in America. Each 16-car consist had a
mixture of roomettes, compartments, bedrooms
and drawings rooms with plenty of dining and
lounging areas.

The *Century* carried not only a barber shop,
but a valet, maid and secretary as well. Master

On trains like the *20th Century*, the privacy and comfort of a roomette, the most talked-of innovation in sleeping accommodations, is available at little more than the cost of an open section. Designed for fastidious living, the roomette contains a luxuriously soft, full-sized bed, concealed toilet facilities, a clothes locker, and such welcome refinements as air conditioning, individualized lighting, ventilation and temperature control.

The famous hospitality of the *20th Century* is nowhere more apparent than in its diner. For here, when you choose to be alone, you can have a table to yourself . . . here, too, when you feel like mingling with people, the opportunity is made each evening. For, after the last meal is served, this magnificently decorated car becomes a night club complete with colored lights, swing music and secluded conversational nooks.

"A visit to the bar lounge of the 20th Century is an experience akin to being a guest in a famous and exclusive club. For rarely does the Century move without a quorum of internationally known people aboard," stated New York Central promotion literature.

NEW YORK CENTRAL'S World-Famous
20ᵀᴴ CENTURY LIMITED
BUILT BY PULLMAN-STANDARD
THE WORLD'S LARGEST BUILDERS OF RAILROAD AND TRANSIT EQUIPMENT

The drawing room on the *20th Century* resembles a living room. One full-sized bed folds into the wall. The sofa and upper also make up into full-sized beds. But when all three beds are made down for the night, ample space remains for moving about. Of course, in the drawing rooms on this magic train, the complete toilet facilities are concealed and, in many instances, adjoining rooms are available.

FOR almost 40 years, the *Twentieth Century Limited* has been one of the most famous and luxurious trains on earth. Today, streamlined into sleek beauty by Pullman-Standard, it has taken on new and even greater significance. For the sight of it flashing over the countryside as silently and majestically as a meteor aptly symbolizes the quiet efficiency with which the railroads of America have set about the task of making modern streamlined transportation available.

In 6 years 16 railroad systems have added Pullman-Standard streamlined units

If you think back, you'll remember that in February 1934 there was but one streamliner in the entire country . . . and that, built by Pullman-Standard, was exhibited at the second opening of Chicago's Century of Progress.

By way of contrast, today practically every major city can boast of this modern service . . . and in practically every section the pleasing and low whistle of these trains has become a familiar sound. For within these six eventful years the

number of railroads operating Pullman-Standard streamlined trains or cars has increased from one to sixteen . . . the number of track miles served by them, extended until they span the country from coast to coast, from Maine to Mexico.

Pullman-Standard streamliners are putting profits back into railroading

As the American creator of this type of transportation, and as the builder of over 70% of the light-weight, streamlined units which have been purchased, Pullman-Standard's role in the achievements of this phenomenal record has been vital. Yet in an important sense it has been secondary to the one which you, a representative of the American traveling public, have played.

By riding these Pullman-Standard-built streamliners in such numbers that you have made them the most popular and profitable trains on earth, you have encouraged the railroads to put an ever-increasing number into service and enabled them to pack a lifetime's advance in safety and comfort, within the limits of six short years.

A visit to the bar lounge of the *20th Century* is an experience akin to being a guest in a famous and exclusive club. For rarely does the *Century* move without a quorum of internationally known people aboard. And, as the social center of this magnificent train, it is here that you will encounter them.

PULLMAN-STANDARD CAR MANUFACTURING COMPANY—CHICAGO
Copyright 1940, by Pullman-Standard Car Manufacturing Company

"Tops" IN STREAMLINERS ARE BUILT BY *Pullman-Standard*

Smooth... is the word for the "CENTURY"

Smooth Ride... The "Century" follows the *only* Water Level Route between East and West. Carefully "manicured" roadbed and finest equipment assure easy, cushioned travel.

Smooth Service... Courteous, especially selected personnel anticipate your every wish. Delicious meals are served in the luxuriously appointed diner or in your own room.

Here's a glimpse of the Fascinating Life aboard the "Century"

From powerful "hooded" locomotive to observation solarium, the 20th Century Limited is a masterpiece of streamlined perfection. To ride it is to treat yourself to a luxurious interlude between one day's duties and the next. It's the train of "who's who in America." Ride it on your next trip between New York and Chicago.

Smooth Sleep... You arrive refreshed and completely rested. All accommodations are spacious, *private* rooms with *extra long*, deep mattressed beds.

THE 20TH CENTURY LIMITED

bedroom patrons could look forward to a hot shower while the Hudson clipped off the distance at 80 mph. Even the mail dropped in its RPO got a special *20th Century Limited* cancellation stamp.

Although most existing streamliners were brightly decorated, the NYC opted for grey flannel suit conservatism. The lounge was decorated with cork wall paneling, grey and rust colored leather furniture and a light grey ceiling with both indirect and spot lighting. A circular foyer/vestibule and the furniture placement visually broke up the natural corridor look of the car.

Each of the two dining cars seated 38 in three distinct areas. The floors were carpeted, while walls were either leather or walnut covered, and the entire area was reflected in various mirrors and glass pier walls. Normal operation required both diners to be coupled together with seating areas back to back.

After the dinner hour, *Century* diners were transformed into night clubs, with lighting dimmed and piped in big-band music. Of course, all meals were served on distinctive *20th Century* china, with matching flatware.

In the *Century*, the best was saved for last: the observation. Seating choices included grey leather sofas or tan pigskin chairs. The bulkhead separating the observation area from the adjacent lounge had an illuminated model of the train's streamlined Hudson displayed in a glass case. Privacy was ensured by venetian blinds, and the front area of the car contained the master bedroom, capable of being opened "en suite" with an adjacent bedroom for maximum luxury.

This paradigm of luxury ran in two sections regularly. Of course, once past the gates at Grand Central Terminal, passengers walked down its fabled red carpet. Alas, the carpet was the only part of this national institution which made it into the Smithsonian. This 260-foot-long broadloom rug exalted patrons to the level of travelers on the fabled *Orient Express*. There was no finer way to go between New York City and Chicago in 16 hours prior to the jet age.

After creating the *Mercury* in its own Beech Grove, Indiana shops, and ordering the *Century* from Pullman, in January, 1941 NYC placed an order with Budd. The Central wanted 32 cars for a new, daily coach/parlor businessman's train across upstate New York to Cleveland and Detroit. It would be christened with an old name: *Empire State Express*.

Perhaps no train of its era was better known than the original *Empire State Express*. Conceived by General Passenger Agent George Daniels, it was originally placed in service with steam locomotives and wooden cars on October 26, 1891.

The name and route dated back to the 19th Century, but certainly not the equipment. Once again, Budd retained the services of Paul Cret and with the assistance of NYC personnel, they created "The World's Finest Day Train." Self-promotion aside, the *Empire State Express* ranked with the finest of coach and parlor service trains.

As delivered, each train set consisted of a mail-baggage, baggage-tavern-lounge, eight coaches, three parlors, two diners and parlor-observation. Once again colors such as mulberry, marine blue and evergreen were accented by fine woods and stainless steel trim. Train capacity was 622 patrons.

The forward lounge was reserved for parlor patrons, but in acknowledgement of its 85% coach loading, both dining cars and the observation lounge were open to all. A very unusual feature was the commissioning of 36 oil paintings of the Hudson Valley and its Dutch Rip Van Winkle heritage. The end bulkheads in every coach, along with the forward bulkhead of the observation, displayed one painting.

The lounge, bar and dining areas were highlighted with carpeted floors, pigskin leather sofas and overstuffed aluminum framed lounge chairs. A full-service circular wet bar was included, faced in Flexwood. Like his previous work, Cret lavished the use of exotic wood veneers throughout the train, particularly on the vertical end walls and bulkheads. This is a trademark of pre-war design, as Formica and other man-made materials took over after 1945.

Although Electro-Motive had confidently proposed diesels to power this magnificent train, Motive Power Chief Paul Kiefer chose his standard 4-6-4 Hudsons. However, #5426 and 5429 got special Dreyfuss treatment which included a bullet nose and the addition of Budd stainless

NEW YORK CENTRAL RAILROAD

★Regularly assigned cars are air-conditioned	Parlor, Sleeping and Dining Car Service—Eastbound	★Regularly assigned cars are air-conditioned

Abbreviations: Sec.—Section; D. R.—Drawing Room; Comp.—Compartment.

No. 2—The Pacemaker—Daily
Luxury All Coach Train—Completely Air-Conditioned
★Club Lounge Chicago to New York (Buffet)
Coaches—*Special coach for women*
★Chicago to New York (Reclining Seat De Luxe)
★Dining Car Chicago to New York
Observation Lounge
★Chicago to New York (Buffet)
All seats reserved and assigned in advance. No extra charge

No. 4—New York Special—Daily
Lounge Cars
★Chicago-Detroit-New York (Buffet) From M. C. No. 44 at Buffalo
★Niagara Falls to New York (6 Double Bedroom-Buffet)
Sleeping Cars
★Chicago to New York (14 Sec.) From No. 14 at Buffalo
★Chicago to New York via Niagara Falls (8 Sec.-D. R.-2 Comp.) In M. C. No. 58 via Welland
★Cincinnati to New York (14 Sec.) From No. 14 at Buffalo
★Detroit to New York (8 Sec.-Lounge) From M. C. No. 44 at Buffalo
★Buffalo to New York (12 Sec.-D. R.)
★Dining Car Chicago to Buffalo—M. C. No. 44
★Coaches Chicago to New York (Reclining Seat De Luxe) From M. C. No. 44 at Buffalo

No. 6—Fifth Avenue Special—Daily
Lounge Car
★Chicago to New York (6 Double Bedroom-Buffet)
Sleeping Cars
★Chicago to New York (10 Roomette-5 Double Bedroom)
★Chicago to New York (12 Sec.-D.R.)
★Chicago to New York (8 Sec.-D. R.-2 Comp.)
★Cleveland to New York (14 Sec.)
★Buffalo to Massena via Utica, Rome and Watertown (12 Sec.-2 Double Bedroom)
★Dining Car serving all meals
★Coach Chicago to New York (Reclining Seat De Luxe)

No. 8—The Wolverine—Daily
Lounge Car
★Chicago to New York (8 Sec.-Buffet)
Sleeping Cars
★Chicago to New York (10 Roomette-5 Double Bedroom)
★Chicago to New York (8 Sec.-D. R.-2 Comp.)
★Chicago to Boston (8 Sec.-D. R.-2 Comp.)
★Detroit to Boston (8 Sec.-5 Double Bedroom)
★Niagara Falls to New York (8 Sec.-4 Double Bedroom)
★Dining Car serving all meals
★Coach Chicago to New York (Reclining Seat De Luxe)
★Albany to Boston

No. 10—The Water Level Limited—Daily
Lounge Car
★Chicago to New York (6 Double Bedroom-Buffet)
Sleeping Cars
★Chicago to New York (10 Roomette-5 Double Bedroom)
★Chicago to New York (4 Comp.-4 Bedroom-2 D. R.)
★Chicago to New York (12 Sec.-D. R.)
★Chicago to New York (6 Sec.-6 Double Bedroom)
★Chicago to Boston (6 Sec.-6 Double Bedroom) In No. 132 from Cleveland; B. & A. No. 10
★Cleveland to New York (6 Sec.-6 Double Bedroom)
★Buffalo to Albany (12 Sec.-D. R.) Open 9.00 p.m.
★Parlor Car Chicago to Cleveland
★Dining Car serving all meals
★Coach Chicago to New York (Reclining Seat De Luxe) (Diner-Lounge)

No. 12—Southwestern Limited—Daily
★Lounge Car St. Louis to New York (Buffet)
Observation Sleeping Car
★St. Louis to New York (D. R.-Comp.-2 Double Bedroom-Buffet)
Sleeping Cars
★St. Louis to New York (10 Roomette-5 Double Bedroom)
★St. Louis to New York (10 Sec.-D. R.-Comp.)
★St. Louis to New York (10 Sec.-2 Double Bedroom-1 Comp.)
★St. Louis to Boston (8 Sec.-D. R.-3 Double Bedroom) In B. & A. No. 8
★Cleveland to New York (17 Roomette)
★Cleveland to New York (6 Sec.-6 Double Bedroom)-Two
★Cleveland to New York (8 Sec.-D. R.-2 Comp.)
★Cleveland to New York (13 Double Bedroom)
★Cleveland to Boston (6 Sec.-6 Double Bedroom) In B. & A. No. 8
★Dining Car serving all meals
★Coach St. Louis to New York (Reclining Seat De Luxe)—Streamlined

No. 14—Interstate Express—Daily
★Lounge Car Chicago to Boston (Buffet)
Sleeping Cars
★Chicago to New York (14 Sec.) In No. 4 from Buffalo
★Chicago to Boston (8 Sec.-D. R.-2 Comp.) } In B. & A.
★Chicago to Boston (8 Sec.-Lounge) } No. 46
★Buffalo to Boston (12 Sec.-D. R.) }
★Cincinnati to New York (14 Sec.) In No. 4 from Buffalo
★Parlor Car Chicago to Buffalo
★Dining Cars Chicago to Buffalo
★Springfield to Boston In B. & A. No. 46
Coaches
★Chicago to New York (Reclining Seat De Luxe) In No. 4 from Buffalo
★Chicago to Boston (Reclining Seat De Luxe) In B. & A. No. 46

No. 18—Number Eighteen—Daily
Sleeping Cars—May be occupied until 8.00 a.m.
★Chicago to Buffalo (12 Sec.-D. R.) From No. 22 at Cleveland
★Cleveland to Buffalo (12 Sec.-D. R.)
Coaches

No. 22—Lake Shore Limited—Daily
Lounge Car
★Chicago to New York (6 Double Bedroom-Buffet)
Sleeping Cars
★Chicago to New York (8 Sec.-D. R.-2 Comp.)
★Chicago to New York (12 Sec.-D. R.)
★Chicago to Boston via B. & A. (12 Sec.-D. R.)
★Chicago to Boston via B. & M. (12 Sec.-D. R.)
★Chicago to Buffalo (12 Sec.-D. R.) In No. 18 from Cleveland. May be occupied until 8.00 a.m.
★St. Louis to New York (12 Sec.-D. R.) From No. 18 at Cleveland
★Cincinnati to New York (12 Sec.-D. R.) From No. 118 at Cleveland
★Cleveland to Syracuse (12 Sec.-D.R.) From No. 132 at Buffalo
★Dining Cars Chicago to Toledo
★Buffalo to New York
★Coach Chicago to New York (Reclining Seat De Luxe)

No. 24—The Knickerbocker—Daily
Lounge Car
★St. Louis to New York (D. R.-2 Comp.-Buffet)
Sleeping Cars
★St. Louis to New York (10 Roomette-5 Double Bedroom)
★St. Louis to New York (12 Sec.-D. R.)
★Cincinnati to New York (10 Sec.-2 Double Bedroom-1 Comp.)
★Cleveland to New York (12 Sec.-D. R.)
★St. Louis to Boston (8 Sec.-D. R.-2 Comp.) In No. 132 from Cleveland; B. & A. No. 10
★Dining Cars St. Louis to Cleveland
★Cincinnati to Cleveland (Diner Lounge)
★Buffalo to New York
Coaches
★St. Louis to New York (Reclining Seat De Luxe)
★Cincinnati to Cleveland (Reclining Seat De Luxe)

No. 26—Twentieth Century Limited—Daily
Completely Air-Conditioned—Streamlined
For special service charges see page 52
★Lounge Car Chicago to New York (Buffet)
Observation Sleeping Car
★Chicago to New York (Master Room-Bedroom-Buffet)
★Sleeping Cars Chicago to New York (18 Roomette)
★Chicago to New York (10 Roomette-5 Bedroom)—Two
★Chicago to New York (4 Comp.-4 Bedroom-2 D. R.)—Three
★Chicago to New York (13 Double Bedroom)—Two
Pullman Cars only; no coach passengers carried
★Dining Car Chicago to New York

No. 28—New England States—Daily
Lounge Car
★Chicago to Boston (6 Double Bedroom-Buffet)
Sleeping Cars
★Chicago to New York (4 Comp.-4 Bedroom-2 D. R.)
★Chicago to New York (10 Roomette-5 Double Bedroom)
★Chicago to Boston (14 Sec.)
Pullman Cars only; no coach passengers carried
★Dining Cars Chicago to Buffalo
★Albany to Boston

No. 30—The Iroquois—Daily
Sleeping Cars
★Buffalo to New York (6 Sec.-6 Double Bedroom)
Buffalo to Albany (12 Sec.-D. R.)
★Rochester to New York (12 Sec.-D. R.)—Two
★Rochester to New York (6 Sec.-5 Double Bedroom)
★Rochester to Boston (12 Sec.-D. R.) In B. & A. No. 46
Coaches

No. 32—Mail—Daily
Sleeping Cars—May be occupied until 7.30 a.m.
★Syracuse to New York, except Saturday (12 Sec.-D. R.) From No. 42 at Albany
★Albany to New York (12 Sec.-D. R.) Open 9.30 p.m.
Coaches

No. 34—The Seneca—Daily
★Parlor Car Syracuse to New York (Sleeper as Parlor Car)
★Lunch Counter Car Utica to New York
★Coach Syracuse to New York

No. 36—The Genesee—Daily
Sleeping Cars—May be occupied until 7.30 a.m.
★Rochester to New York (12 Sec.-D. R.) In Auburn Road No. 18
★Syracuse to New York (8 Sec.-3 Double Bedroom) Open at 10.00 p.m.
★Utica to New York (12 Sec.-D. R.) Open at 9.30 p.m.
★Oswego to New York except Sat. (12 Sec.-D. R.) From No. 336 at Syracuse
Coaches

No. 38—Missourian—Daily
Lounge Car
★St. Louis to New York via Big Four (8 Sec.-Buffet)
Sleeping Cars
★St. Louis to New York via Big Four (8 Sec.-5 Double Bedroom)
★Chicago to Buffalo (12 Sec.-D. R.) From No. 80 at Cleveland
Parlor Car
★Buffalo to Boston In B. & A. No. 40
★Dining car serving all meals
★Coaches St. Louis to New York (Reclining Seat De Luxe)
★Buffalo to Boston (Reclining Seat De Luxe) In B. & A. No. 40

No. 40—North Shore Limited—Daily
★Lounge Car Chicago to New York via M. C. (Buffet)
Sleeping Cars
★Chicago to New York via M. C. (8 Sec.-4 Double Bedroom)
★Chicago to New York via M. C. (8 Sec.-D. R.-2 Comp.)
★Chicago to Boston via M. C. (12 Sec.-D. R.)
★Parlor Car Buffalo to New York
★Dining Car serving all meals
★Coach Chicago to New York via M. C. (Reclining Seat De Luxe)
★Albany to Boston (Reclining Seat De Luxe)

No. 42—Boston Express—Daily
Sleeping Cars
★Buffalo to Boston (10 Sec.-Lounge)
★Buffalo to Boston (8 Sec.-5 Single Bedroom)
Parlor Car (Restaurant Lounge)
★Toledo to Albany From No. 52 at Buffalo
Dining Car
★Toledo to Albany (Restaurant Lounge)
Coaches

No. 50—Empire State Express—Daily Except Sunday
★Club Lounge Car Buffalo to New York (Buffet)
★Parlor Car Buffalo to New York—Two
★Parlor Car Buffalo to New York (Observation)
★Dining Car Buffalo to New York
★Coach Buffalo to New York (Reclining Seat De Luxe)

No. 52—Buffalo Express—Daily
★Parlor Car Toledo to Albany (Restaurant Lounge)
Coaches

No. 54—The Mohawk—Daily
★Parlor Car Syracuse to New York (Sleeper as Parlor Car)
★Dining Car Syracuse to New York—Diner Lounge
★Coach Buffalo to New York

No. 58—The Niagara—Daily
★Lounge Car Buffalo to Albany (Buffet)
★Parlor Car Buffalo to New York (Sleeper as Parlor Car)
★Coach Buffalo to New York

No. 66—The Grand Central—Daily
Lounge Car
★Chicago to New York (6 Double Bedroom-Buffet)—Two
Sleeping Cars
★Chicago to New York (18 Roomette)—Two
★Chicago to New York (4 Comp.-4 Bedroom-2 D.R.)—Two
★Chicago to New York (14 Sec.)—Two
Pullman cars only; no coach passengers carried.
★Dining Car Chicago to New York

No. 68—The Commodore Vanderbilt—Daily
Lounge Car
★Chicago to New York (6 Double Bedroom-Buffet)
Sleeping Cars
★Chicago to New York (10 Roomette-5 Double Bedroom)
★Chicago to New York (18 Roomette)
★Chicago to New York (4 Comp.-4 Bedroom-2 D.R.)
★Chicago to New York (13 Double Bedroom)
★Chicago to New York (14 Sec.)
Pullman Cars only; no coach passengers carried
★Dining Car Chicago to New York

No. 80—The Maumee—Daily
Sleeping Car
★Chicago to Buffalo (12 Sec.-D. R.) In No. 38 from Cleveland
Coaches

No. 82—The Ontarian—Daily
Sleeping Cars Open 9.00 p.m.
★Buffalo to New York (8 Sec.-D. R.-2 Comp.)
★Buffalo to New York (10 Roomette-5 Double Bedroom)
Pullman cars only; no coach passengers carried

No. 90—The Forest City—Daily
Lounge Cars
★Chicago to New York (8 Sec.-Buffet)
★Chicago to Cleveland (D. R.-Single Bedroom-Buffet)
Sleeping Cars Open 9.30 p.m. Central Time
★Chicago to New York (8 Sec.-D. R.-2 Comp.)
★Chicago to Cleveland Ex. Sat. (17 Roomette)
★Chicago to Cleveland (13 Double Bedroom)
★Chicago to Cleveland (12 Sec.-D. R.)
★Chicago to Cleveland (6 Sec.-6 Double Bedroom)
★Chicago to Cleveland (14 Sec.)—Two
★Chicago to Cleveland (8 Sec.-D. R.-2 Comp.)
★Chicago to Toledo (12 Sec.-D. R.) Open until 8.00 a.m.
★Parlor Car Cleveland to New York
Dining Cars
★Cleveland to Buffalo-Diner Lounge
★Buffalo to New York
Coach
★Chicago to New York (Reclining Seat De Luxe)

No. 96—New York Express—Sunday only
★Club Lounge Car Buffalo to New York (Buffet)
★Parlor Car Buffalo to New York (Observation)
★Parlor Car Buffalo to New York
★Dining Car Buffalo to New York
★Coach Buffalo to New York (Reclining Seat De Luxe)

No. 132—Henry Hudson—Daily
Lounge Car
★Syracuse to New York (Buffet)
Sleeping Cars
★St. Louis to Boston (8 Sec.-D. R.-2 Comp.) From Big Four No. 24; In B. & A. No. 10
★Chicago to Boston (6 Sec.-6 Double Bedroom) From No. 10 at Cleveland; In B. & A. No. 10
★Cleveland to Syracuse (12 Sec.-D. R.) In No. 22 from Buffalo Open 9.30 p.m.
★Cleveland to Toronto (12 Sec.-D. R.) In T. H. & B. No. 71 Open 9.30 p.m.
Dining Cars
★Syracuse to New York (Diner-Lounge)
★Albany to Boston
★Coaches Toledo to New York
★Albany to Boston In B. & A. No. 10

NEW YORK CENTRAL RAILROAD

Main Line—Chicago to Cleveland, Buffalo, Boston and New York

(The time given is Eastern Standard Time Bryan and east and Central Standard Time at stations west of Bryan)

Mls.	Table 2	52-42 D'ly	32 D'ly	44-30 D'ly	14 D'ly	608 D'ly	6 D'ly	82 D'ly	76 D'ly	132 D'ly	2 D'ly	12 D'ly	66 D'ly	8 D'ly	68 D'ly	28 D'ly	26 D'ly	24 D'ly	10 D'ly	142 D'ly	614 D'ly	22 D'ly	88 D'ly	80 D'ly	40 D'ly	38 D'ly	90 D'ly	60 D'ly	78 D'ly	50 Ex. Sun.	96 Sun. only	56 D'ly
	N. Y. C. R. R.	AM	AM	PM	AM	AM	AM	PM	PM	AM	PM	PM	PM	AM	PM	PM	PM	PM	PM	AM	PM	PM	AM	PM	AM	AM	PM	AM	PM	PM	PM	PM
0.0	Lv CHICAGO....(C.T.) (La Salle St. Sta.)	....	1 15	....	9 50	8 30	11 30	....	....	11 40	2 00	....	2 30	....	3 00	3 00	4 00	....	4 05	....	....	5 30	....	8 45	....	....	11 50	....	10 50	....	....	....
6.7	" Englewood	....	....	....	g1002	g8 42	g1142	....	....	g1152	g2 12	....	g 242	....	g3 12	g3 12	g4 12	....	g4 17	....	....	g5 42	....	g8 57	....	....	g1202	....	g1102	....	....	....
26.2	" Gary	....	1 54	....	j1023	9 15	12 06	....	....	12 29	....	....	q 302	....	....	....	....	....	j4 37	....	....	p6 06	....	9 22	....	....	....	....	11 32	....	....	....
58.8	" La Porte	....	2 35	....	....	9 52	12 40	....	....	1 20	....	....	....	....	....	....	....	....	....	....	....	6 42	....	9 56	....	....	....	....	12 20	....	....	....
85.5	" South Bend	....	3 20	....	11 18	10 25	1 10	....	....	2 10	e3 23	....	....	....	q4 25	q4 25	....	....	5 35	....	....	7 12	....	10 28	....	....	w116	....	1 15	....	....	....
89.5	" Mishawaka	....	3 47	....	....	10 33	1 19	....	Leaves Detroit at 5.30 p.m.	2 22	....	....	....	....	....	....	....	....	....	....	....	q7 20	....	e1034	....	....	....	....	1 30	....	....	....
100.6	" Elkhart	4 30	4 20	....	11 45	10 55	1 40	....		2 50	e3 41	....	4 13	....	4 43	g4 43	....	....	5 58	....	6 00	7 43	....	10 54	....	....	1 40	....	1 55	....	....	....
110.5	" Goshen	Via Old Road See Table 41	4 37	....	....	11 10	1 53	....		3 05	....	....	....	....	....	....	....	....	....	....	Via Old Road See Table 41	8 00	....	....	....	....	....	....	2 12	....	....	....
125.7	" Ligonier		5 01	....	....	11 29	....	....		3 26	....	....	....	....	....	....	....	....	....	....		8 23	....	....	....	....	....	....	....	....	....	....
142.2	" Kendallville		5 28	....	....	11 49	ve	....		3 52	....	....	....	....	....	....	....	....	....	....		8 43	....	....	....	....	....	....	2 57	....	....	....
154.9	" Waterloo		5 48	....	....	12 05	2 38	....		4 12	....	....	....	....	....	....	....	....	j6 46	....		9 01	....	j1142	....	....	....	....	b3 12	....	....	....
162.8	" Butler		†5 57	....	....	†1213	....	....		4 22	....	....	....	....	....	....	....	....	....	....		....	....	....	....	....	....	....	....	....	....	....
180.0	" Bryan..........E.T.		7 25	....	....	1 35	4 05	....		5 53	....	....	....	....	....	....	....	....	....	....		10 32	....	....	....	....	....	....	....	....	....	....
233.6	Ar Toledo	9 35	8 45	....	2 50	2 35	5 00	....		7 35	6 40	....	7 15	....	7 45	....	....	....	9 06	....	11 00	11 34	....	2 02	....	....	4 43	....	5 45	....	....	....
233.6	Lv Toledo	9 45	AM	....	2 55	3 00	5 05	....	6 30	8 40	6 40	....	7 15	....	7 45	g7 45	g8 28	....	9 11	....	....	11 47	2 13	2 45	....	....	4 53	....	6 15	....	....	....
267.5	" Port Clinton	10 26	....	....	....	3 40	....	....	....	9 18	....	....	....	....	....	....	....	....	....	....	....	....	....	....	....	....	....	....	7 20	....	....	....
280.4	" Sandusky	10 47	....	....	....	3 59	5 55	....	....	9 38	....	....	....	....	....	....	....	....	....	....	....	....	....	3 38	....	....	5 49	....	7 50	....	....	....
315.0	" Elyria	11 28	....	....	....	4 45	6 32	....	....	10 15	....	....	....	....	....	....	....	....	....	....	....	....	....	4 16	....	....	vp	....	8 47	....	....	....
328.1	" Berea	....	....	....	....	....	....	....	....	....	....	....	....	....	....	....	....	....	....	....	....	....	....	....	....	....	....	....	9 10	....	....	....
334.2	" Linndale	11 59	....	....	4 47	5 15	6 57	....	8 06	10 42	....	....	....	....	....	....	....	....	10 47	....	18 D'ly	1 39	....	4 45	....	....	6 57	....	9 20	....	....	....
340.2	Ar Cleveland (Un. Term.)	12 18	....	....	5 05	h5 33	7 15	....	8 20	11 00	....	....	....	....	....	....	....	....	11 05	....	AM	1 57	k4 18	5 05	....	....	7 15	....	9 40	....	....	....
340.2	Lv Cleveland (Un. Term.)	12 30		4 00	5 45	....	7 25	....	....	11 25	....	8 40	....	....	....	....	....	10 52	11 16	....	2 15	2 10	AM	AM	....	5 36	7 25	8 30	....	....	....	....
347.2	" East Cleveland	12 39	84 D'ly	4 09	5 54	....	7 34	Pullman cars only	....	11 34	....	8 49	....	....	....	....	....	....	11 25	....	2 24	....	....	....	....	5 45	7 34	8 39	....	....	....	....
371.4	" Painesville	1 19		4 52	6 36	....	8 16		The Mercury	bp	....	....	....	....	....	....	....	....	....	....	3 06	....	....	....	....	....	v8 12	9 22	....	....	....	....
387.5	" Geneva	....	PM	5 16	6 54	....	....			....	....	....	....	....	....	....	....	....	....	....	....	....	....	....	....	....	....	9 51	....	....	....	....
396.8	" Ashtabula	1 43	8 05	5 32	7 05	....	....			bp	....	....	....	....	....	....	....	....	....	....	3 47	....	....	....	....	....	v8 36	10 06	....	....	....	....
410.1	" Conneaut	2 00	8 22	5 49	....	....	....			....	....	....	....	....	....	....	....	....	....	....	....	....	....	....	....	....	....	10 24	....	....	....	....
422.3	" North Girard	....	....	6 09	....	....	....			....	....	....	....	....	....	....	....	....	....	....	....	....	....	....	....	....	....	10 41	....	....	....	....
437.6	" Erie	2 35	8 55	6 35	7 50	....	9 23			1 33	....	....	Pullman Cars only	....	Pullman cars only	Pullman cars only	Pullman cars only	....	1 07	....	4 55	....	....	....	....	7 21	9 18	11 06	....	....	....	....
451.6	" North East	2 50	....	6 55	....	....	....			....	....	....		....				....	....	....	....	....	....	....	....	....	....	11†24	....	....	....	....
467.1	" Westfield	3 15	9 27	7 21	8 26		....			....	....	....		....				....	....	....	5 30	....	....	....	....	7 56	9 49	11 42	....	....	....	....
484.3	" Dunkirk	3 40	9 50	7 50	8 50	4	....			....	....	....		....				....	....	....	5 55	....	....	....	....	8 17	....	12 07	....	....	....	....
525.3	Ar Buffalo (Cent. Term.)	4 50	10 43	8 52	9 40	Daily	11 00	....		3 05	11 35	11 59	12 10	....	12 40	....	....	2 02	2 38	....	6 53	5 30	54 D'ly	58 Daily	....	9 06	10 55	1 05	....	....	....	....
552.2	Ar Niagara Falls	6 08	....	9 55	....	PM	....	....		....	....	....	....	....	....	....	....	....	....	....	7 54	....	AM	AM	....	10 15	12 20	3 35	....	....	....	....
525.3	Lv Buffalo (Cent. Term.)	5 05		9 10	9 54	10 10	11 05	11 25		3 19	11 35	....	....	12 20	....	....	....	2 02	2 38	1 44	....	5 45	5 54	7 50	9 24	9 34	11 05	....		1 30	1 30	2 37
558.8	" Batavia	5 49		9 51	....	10 51	....	....		....	....	....	....	....	....	....	....	....	....	2 25	....	....	6 55	8 31	....	10 14	11 45	....		....	....	3 18
591.3	Ar Rochester	6 25	36 Daily	10 25	11 03	11 27	12 17	....		4 28	....	....	....	x1 28	....	....	....	....	....	2 57	....	6 55	7 53	9 03	10 30	10 46	12 17	....	34 D'ly	2 35	2 39	3 51
613.8	" Palmyra	....		....	....	....	....	....		....	....	....	....	....	....	....	....	....	....	3 57	....	....	8 31	....	....	....	....	....		....	....	....
621.2	" Newark	7 11	PM	11 21	....	....	....	....		....	....	....	....	....	....	....	....	....	....	4 08	....	....	8 43	9 48	....	....	....	....	PM	....	....	4 30
626.7	" Lyons	7 21	....	11 31	....	....	....	....		....	....	....	....	....	....	....	....	....	....	....	....	....	8 54	9 58	....	....	....	....	....	....	....	4 40
671.6	" Syracuse	8 10	11 10	12 17	12 34	1 00	1 47	b2 05	All seats on the Mercury are reserved, individually assigned in advance and sold by number	6 00	....	b2 34	....	2 56	....	....	....	4 35	5 10	4 57	....	8 25	9 46	10 43	11 54	12 10	1 42	....	1 55	3 58	4 08	5 25
676.3	" East Syracuse	....	....	....	....	....	....	....		....	....	....	....	....	....	....	....	....	....	5 33	....	....	....	....	....	....	....	....	....	....	....	....
692.4	" Canastota	8 45	11 37	....	....	....	....	....		....	....	....	....	....	....	....	....	....	....	6 03	....	....	10 18	....	....	....	....	....	2 18	....	....	....
697.6	" Oneida	8 56	11 49	....	....	....	....	....		6 39	....	....	....	....	....	....	....	....	....	6 16	....	....	10 30	....	....	....	....	....	2 28	....	....	6 06
710.7	" Rome	9 17	12 10	....	....	....	....	....		6 55	The Pacemaker	....	....	....	The Commodore Vanderbilt	New England States	Twentieth Century Limited	....	....	6 41	....	....	10 49	11 43	12 39	....	....	....	2 46	....	4 54	6 23
724.5	" Utica	9 34	12 30	1 25	1 35	1 59	2 44	....		7 12		....	....	....				....	....	7 02	....	9 23	11 06	12 00	12 56	1 11	2 34	....	3 03	4 51	5 11	6 40
738.5	" Herkimer	10 03	....	....	....	....	....	....		7 33		....	....	....				....	....	7 42	....	....	11 36	....	....	....	....	....	3 31	....	....	....
745.5	" Little Falls	10 18	....	....	....	....	....	....		7 43		....	....	....				....	....	7 55	....	....	11 49	....	....	....	....	....	3 42	....	....	....
761.2	" Fort Plain	10f38	....	....	....	....	....	....		....		....	....	....				....	....	8 16	....	....	12 09	....	....	....	....	....	4 05	....	....	....
764.2	" Palatine Bridge	10f46	....	....	....	....	....	....		8 06		....	....	....				....	....	8 22	....	....	12 17	....	....	....	....	....	4 11	....	....	s7 28
775.7	" Fonda	11 04	....	....	....	....	....	....		8 22		....	The Grand Central	....				....	....	8 41	....	....	12 34	....	....	....	....	....	4 28	....	....	7 43
786.3	" Amsterdam	11 19	....	....	....	....	....	....		8 36		....		....				....	....	8 59	....	....	....	....	....	....	....	....	4 46	....	....	7 58
802.1	" Schenectady	11 44	2 34	....	....	....	....	....		9 00		....		....		....		....	7 13	9 22	....	10 45	1 11	1 29	....	2 30	3 57	....	5 10	....	6 37	8 19
819.0	Ar Albany	12 10	3 05	3 32	3 22	3 55	4 35	....		9 25	y4 38	b5 00	....	5 24	....	5 45	b6 02	7 09	7 42	9 50	....	11 11	1 38	1 53	2 36	2 54	4 20	....	5 38	6 35	7 03	8 42
	B. & A. R. R.	42		46	46	44	8			10	8	8		8		28		10	10			22			40	40	14				42	42
819.0	Lv Albany	1 00	....	3 45	3 45	4 50	5 40	....		9 40	5 40	5 40	....	5 40	....	6 08	....	9 40	9 40	....	....	11 26	....	....	3 15	3 15	5 20	....	....		1 00	1 00
842.2	Ar Chatham	1 37	....	....	....	....	....	....		a1012	....	....	....	....	....	....	....	a1012	a1012	....	....	12 00	....	....	3 49	3 49	6 05	....	....		1 37	1 37
868.8	" Pittsfield	2 25	....	5 10	5 10	6 05	6 49	....		10 50	6 49	6 49	....	6 49	....	7 16	....	10 50	10 50	....	....	12 38	....	....	4 39	4 39	6 57	....	....		2 25	2 25
921.1	" Springfield	3 50	....	6 40	6 40	7 47	8 13	....		12 20	8 13	8 13	....	8 13	....	8 36	....	12 20	12 20	....	....	2 05	....	....	6 10	6 10	8 26	....	....		3 50	3 50
975.1	" Worcester	5 18	....	8 00	8 00	9 13	9 30	....		1 38	9 30	9 30	....	9 30	....	9 53	....	1 38	1 38	....	....	3 23	....	....	7 34	7 34	10 09	....	....		5 18	5 18
1011.3	" Newtonville	....	....	8 55	8 55	....	10 25	....		2 30	10 25	10 25	....	10 25	....	10 43	....	2 30	2 30	....	....	4 15	....	....	8 25	8 25	11 09	....	....		....	....
1019.4	Ar BOSTON	6 30	....	9 10	9 10	10 28	10 40	....	168	2 45	10 40	10 40	....	10 40	....	10 58	....	2 45	2 45	....	....	4 30	....	....	8 40	8 40	11 25	....	....		6 30	6 30
	(South Sta.)	AM		AM	AM	AM	AM		D'ly	PM	AM	AM		AM		AM		PM	PM			PM			PM	PM	PM				AM	AM
	N. Y. C. R. R.								AM	AM																						
819.0	Lv Albany	1 05	3 18	3 51	4 12	4 12	4 35	....	8 10	9 45		....	....	5 24	....	....		7 09	7 42	10 05	....	11 23	1 50	2 05	2 45	3 02	4 29	....	5 52	6 35	7 08	8 55
847.5	Ar Hudson	1 44	3 57	....	....	....	....	....	8 59	....		....	....	....	....	....		....	....	10 37	....	....	....	2 38	....	....	....	....	6 24	....	....	9 29
851.8	" Greendale	....	....	....	....	....	....	....	9 07	....		....	....	....	....	....		....	....	10 44	....	....	....	....	....	....	....	....	....	....	....	....
867.2	" Barrytown	....	....	....	....	....	....	....	9 39	....		....	....	....	....	....		....	....	11 07	....	....	....	....	....	....	....	....	....	....	....	....
872.8	" Rhinecliff	....	....	....	....	....	....	....	9 50	....		....	....	....	....	....		....	....	11 15	....	....	2 48	....	....	....	....	....	6 51	....	....	9 57
882.7	" Hyde Park	....	....	....	....	....	....	....	10 05	....	Luxury All Coach Train	....	....	....	....	....		....	....	....	....	....	....	....	....	....	....	....	....	....	....	....
888.4	" Poughkeepsie	2 26	4 42	....	5 25	5 25	5 46	....	10 13	10 55		n6 17	....	6 40	....	....	Special service charge	....	....	11 47	....	12 39	3 09	3 21	....	4 10	....	....	7 10	....	....	10 17
902.9	" Beacon	....	....	5 32	5 49	5 49	6 07	....	10 34	....		....	....	....	....	....		....	....	12 14	....	12 58	....	3 40	....	....	....	....	7 29	....	....	10 38
909.4	" Cold Spring	....	....	....	....	....	....	....	10 44	....		....	....	....	....	....		....	....	12 25	....	....	....	....	....	....	....	....	7 39	....	....	....
912.1	" Garrison	....	....	....	....	....	....	....	10 50	....		....	....	....	....	....		....	....	12 31	....	....	....	a3 51	....	....	....	....	....	....	....	....
920.6	" Peekskill	....	5 30	....	....	....	....	....	11 03	....		....	....	....	....	....		....	....	12 48	....	....	....	4 03	....	....	....	....	7 56	....	....	11 02
928.5	" Harmon	3 33	5 44	b6 14	b6 31	b6 31	b6 44	b6 48	11 14	b1142	b6 59	b7 04	b7 30	b7 35	b8 08	....	b8 00	b9 06	b9 39	1 03	....	b1 33	b3 57	4 14	b4 37	4 55	b6 20	....	8 07	b8 35	b9 05	11 14
931.0	" Ossining	3 45	....	....	....	....	....	....	....	....	....	....	....	....	....	....	....	....	....	1 11	....	....	....	....	....	....	....	....	....	....	....	....
936.7	" Tarrytown	3 55	....	....	....	....	....	....	....	....	....	....	....	....	....	....	....	....	....	1 19	....	....	....	....	....	....	....	....	....	....	....	....
946.7	" Yonkers	4 13	6 11	b6 42	c6 59	c6 59	....	....	....	....	....	....	....	....	....	....	....	....	....	1 32	....	....	....	b4 41	....	....	....	....	....	....	....	b1141
957.0	" New York (125th St.)	b4 33	b6 33	b7 03	....	....	....	....	11b57	....	....	....	....	....	....	....	....	....	....	1 53	....	....	b4 42	b5 01	b5 22	b5 38	b7 03	....	b8 49	b9 16	b9 49	b1159
961.2	Ar NEW YORK	4 45	6 45	7 15	7 30	7 30	7 40	7 45	12 08	12 35	8 00	8 00	8 30	8 30	9 00	....	9 00	9 59	10 30	2 05	....	2 30	4 53	5 10	5 30	5 50	7 15	....	9 00	9 25	10 00	12 10
	(Grand Cent. Term.)	AM	AM	AM	AM	AM	AM	AM	PM	PM	AM	AM	AM	AM	AM	AM	AM	AM	AM	PM	AM	PM	PM	PM	PM	PM	PM	PM	PM	PM	PM	AM

REFERENCE NOTES

For Parlor, Sleeping and Dining Car Service, see pages 9 and 10.

All A.M. time is given in light figures. **All P.M. time in heavy figures.**

- † Daily, except Sunday.
- a Stops Sunday only.
- b Stops only to discharge passengers.
- c Stops to discharge passengers from Utica and beyond.
- d Stops on signal to receive passengers for New York.
- e Stops on signal to receive passengers for Toledo and beyond.
- f Stops on signal to receive or discharge passengers.
- g Stops on signal to receive passengers.
- h Through cars for Pittsburgh arrive Erie R. R. station at 5.35 p.m.
- j Stops to receive or discharge passengers for or from Cleveland and beyond.
- k Arrives Erie R. R. station.
- n Stops on signal to discharge passengers from points west of Buffalo.
- o Stops on signal to receive passengers for New York and Boston.
- p Stops on signal to receive passengers for Buffalo and beyond.
- q Stops on signal to receive passengers for points beyond Albany.
- r Pullman cars only.
- s Makes regular stop Sundays. Stops week-days to discharge passengers from Rochester and stations beyond.
- v Stops to discharge passengers from Chicago and beyond.
- w Stops on signal to receive sleeping car passengers for Columbus, Ohio.
- x Stops to discharge passengers or to receive passengers for New York.
- y Stops to discharge passengers from Toledo and beyond.

NYC September 29, 1940 timetable

*The news about Pearl Harbor
dampened enthusiasm for the
inaugural run of the new*
Empire State Express *on
December 7, 1941.*

steel side panels beginning over the drivers and
flowing backward across the tender continuously
into the cars themselves. Full-width diaphragms
completed the seamless impression, especially at
speed. A special black and silver paint scheme
was applied to the non-stainless portions of the
locomotives.

Equipment delays and defense mobilization
postponed the planned debut of the *Empire State
Express* past its October 26, 1941 50th anniversary. Finally, all was ready. The inaugural service
was planned for a Sunday to get maximum press,
and Ed Nowak, NYC's photographer, spent
countless hours trackside and in his darkroom.
Spotless, on time and in the full glare of anticipated publicity, twin streamliners simultaneously left
Detroit and New York City on a bright Sunday,
December 7, 1941. Of course, the news from
Pearl Harbor stunned the revelers into silence and
reduced the anticipated coverage from the first
page to second section news. It was the last pre-
war train.

Wartime kept the Central's great steel fleet
loaded for the next five years. Streamliners would
not have a chance to age gracefully, just keep
rolling for the duration. Gasoline and rubber
rationing ensured that all passenger cars the railroads could find and make suitable for service
would be quickly filled.

A KNIGHT IN SHINING ARMOR:
READING'S *CRUSADER*

Although in general thought of as a coal-hauler,
not a passenger road, the Reading Railroad
willingly played second fiddle to no one. With
the PRR grabbing the bulk of the NYC-Philadel-
phia traffic, and the B&O's *Royal Blue* contend-
ing for the rest, Reading needed a spectacular
entry into the streamliner competition.

Behold, on December 13, 1937 Reading's
knight in shining armor appeared. Literally clad in
stainless steel, from pilot to observation, Reading
joined the East Coast fray with its *Crusader* service between Jersey City (a ferry ride away from
Wall Street) and Philadelphia.

The 5-car train was Shotwelded of stainless
steel and in a most unusual fashion was bi-directional. Since it made two roundtrips per day on
the 90-mile run, turning the train was only extra
work. Each end began with an observation-

Otto Kuhler designed the Lehigh Valley's streamlined Pacifics used to pull The John Wilkes; the train's first trip occurred June 4, 1939. The train ran between Pittston/Wilkes-Barre, Pennsylvania and New York City.

The 1940 Pennsylvania's South Wind (Chicago to Miami) was painted in PRR's tuscan red. It ran via Louisville, then over the Louisville & Nashville to Montgomery where the Atlantic Coast Line then picked it up.

An early view of inside the EMC diesel building plant at La Grange, Illinois. In this erecting bay, early switchers are in the foreground while a long, sleek B&O E unit sits on the plant floor behind.

lounge, connected to a coach-smoker, and finally the diner-tavern was the center car. In deference to its Wall Street patronage, even the diner-tavern had overhead luggage racks—designed to hold attache' cases.

Since it was truly a commuter's train, even Paul Cret was limited in his design parameters, sticking to leather seats, colorful pastels and floral drapes in the tavern-lounge. However, breakfasts created in the diner-tavern each morning were equaled only by the manhattans and martinis consumed in the late afternoon, according to Lucius Beebe.

The *Crusader's* motive power was a medium 4-6-2 Pacific locomotive. However, Cret streamlined it with the application of a stainless steel "bathtub" shroud. The shroud was rather ordinary, but the use of the stainless steel Budd fluting from the boiler front back along the tender to the car sides was revolutionary. It was quite distinctive, and would reappear with Cret's streamlining of the NYC *Empire State Express* Hudsons four years later.

The *Crusader* ping-ponged its way between Jersey City and Philadelphia unremarked until the end of WWII. The Budd-built equipment was still

An early EMD-built E-3 #822 demonstrator diesel unit sported silver trucks and underbody.

in excellent shape, and by then the tired steamer was replaced by a diesel. Finally, in 1963 the cars were sold to the Canadian National, where they served until the early 1980s.

THE FLEET OF MODERNISM: PENNSY'S FINEST

In early 1934, just as the finishing touches were being put on the *Pioneer Zephyr* and the *M-10000*, the Pennsylvania was about to enter the streamlined era in its own way, not yet with a fleet of cars, but with just a locomotive: its memorable GG-1 electric.

Straining under the weight of the Depression, even the mighty Pennsy—for years the largest corporation in the world—completed its New York to Washington electrification only on the strength of New Deal RFC loans. An integral part of that master plan was a new, 4,620 hp electric locomotive to haul Pennsy's finest.

Designated the GG-1, the first engine arrived in August, 1934 from Baldwin, riveted together in the best steam locomotive tradition. The PRR was awed by its power, but the packaging needed improvement. Raymond Loewy was the answer. Loewy re-arranged some details, applied the famous "catwhisker" five-pinstripe scheme and ordered the body arc-welded together instead of riveted. Voila! It was perhaps the all-time classic North American electric locomotive in terms of design and performance combined. Not many pieces of equipment keep going for virtually a half-century, but the GG-1 did—at speeds of 80 mph or better.

Impressed by his GG-1 accomplishments, the PRR authorized Loewy to design its abuilding 1938 *Broadway Limited*. As Pennsy's finest, it had to compete head-to-head with rival NYC's *20th Century Limited*, also planned to debut on June 15, 1938. Loewy grasped the challenge, while Cret assisted with the interior appointments.

Pullman-Standard received an order for 52 new cars to equip the 1938 *Broadway*. The PRR rebuilt the necessary headend cars and diners at its massive Altoona shops to keep some work in house. No new locomotives were ordered for the Fleet of Modernism.

The *Broadway* was always powered under the wires with a Loewy designed GG-1, but such was

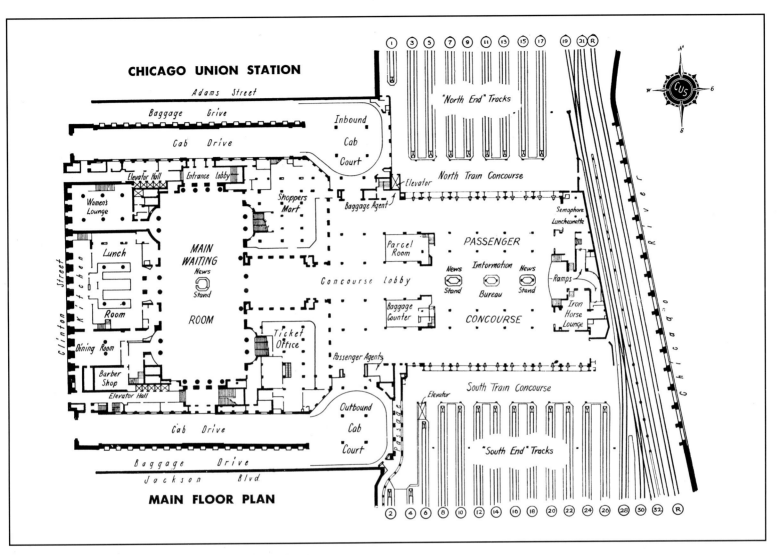

CHICAGO UNION STATION

MAIN FLOOR PLAN

Adams Street

Baggage Drive

Cab Drive

Inbound Cab Court

"North End" Tracks

① ③ ⑤ ⑦ ⑨ ⑪ ⑬ ⑮ ⑰ ⑲ ㉑ Ⓡ

North Train Concourse

Clinton Street

Elevator Hall — Entrance Lobby

Women's Lounge

Shoppers Mart

Elevator

Baggage Agent

Lunch Room

MAIN WAITING ROOM

News Stand

Parcel Room

Semaphore

Luncheonette

PASSENGER

Concourse Lobby

News Stand — Information Bureau — News Stand

Ramps

Dining Room

Ticket Office

Baggage Counter

CONCOURSE

Iron Horse Lounge

Barber Shop

Elevator Hall

Passenger Agents

Elevator

South Train Concourse

Outbound Cab Court

Cab Drive

Baggage Drive

Jackson Blvd.

"South End" Tracks

Chicago River

② ④ ⑥ ⑧ ⑩ ⑫ ⑭ ⑯ ⑱ ⑳ ㉒ ㉔ ㉖ ㉘ ㉚ ㉜ Ⓡ

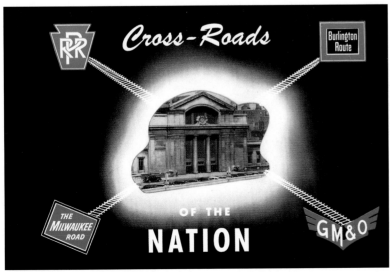

Cross-Roads OF THE NATION

PRR — Burlington Route — THE MILWAUKEE ROAD — GM&O

"Crossroads of the Nation" was the Chicago Union Station's slogan. Standing majestically on the Chicago River at the edge of the famous Loop district, the $90 million structure was constructed of stone, steel and concrete. It contained 35 acres and when built, more than 1,500 employees worked there. Work was largely completed by 1925. The station served the Pennsylvania, the CB&Q, the Milwaukee Road and the Gulf, Mobile & Ohio.

149

A New Train St. Louis to Chicago

The Blue Bird

4:25 PM

The Blue Bird from Chicago to St. Louis leaves Dearborn Station 4:30 pm. Same equipment, same schedule as its predecessor "St. Louis Special". Four hours 55 minutes to Delmar Station, St. Louis . . . 20 minutes more to Union Station. All Wabash trains to and from Chicago stop at Englewood Station, 63rd and Wallace Streets, which serves the entire South Side.

All Wabash trains to and from St. Louis stop at Delmar Station, 6001 Delmar Boulevard, the center of the busy West End district. It's a great convenience if you are going to or from any place in St. Louis west of Grand Ave.

A train of exquisite beauty, blue and gold outside (like the famous Banner Blue) . . . luxury and comfort inside . . . decorated in blue-greens, creams, grays, and rust . . . touches of chromium highlights in the new, ultra-modern design of the furnishings. A beautiful parlor-lounge car, curtained and carpeted as a spacious living room . . . a dining car with venetian blinds, glistening silver, spotless linens . . . and excellent meals perfectly served. One of the smartest and most modern of all standard trains.

THE SCHEDULE

Leave St. Louis, Union Station	. . . . .	4:25 pm
Leave St. Louis, Delmar Station	. . . .	4:39 pm
Arrive Chicago, Englewood	. . . . . .	9:23 pm
Arrive Chicago, Dearborn Station	. . . .	9:35 pm

Ideal as the "Home Run" train for persons returning from St. Louis to their homes in Chicago.

The December 12, 1938 Wabash timetable shows the Blue Bird leaving St. Louis at 4:25 p.m. in time for a Chicago arrival at 9:35 p.m. that same evening. Although not streamlined, it was one of the "smartest and most modern of all standard trains."

The Crusader, *which ran between New York and Philadelphia, featured tail lounge, rear observation lounge car, and all cars were air-conditioned. No extra fares were charged for any of the train's seating accommodations.*

Interior of the Crusader *dining car created a cozy atmosphere with linen tablecloths, heavy silverware and good china plates and cups. And, of course, meals were delicious.*

not the case elsewhere. Although Loewy shrouded a total of three PRR K4 4-6-2 Pacific locomotives, none were specifically allotted to the *Broadway*. Streamlined #3768 pulled the inaugural train eastbound from Chicago and was part of that equipment pool, however. Loewy also did the PRR's 4-4-4-4 Duplex engines and its experimental 6-4-4-6 "Big Engine" as displayed at the 1939-40 World's Fair in New York's Flushing Meadows. All were visually distinctive, but none had the longevity or performance of the GG-1.

Of special note was the mid-train sleeper-lounge, containing two bedrooms, shower, barber shop and a secretary's office. The main lounge was paneled in harewood and included an oval mirror plus murals of NYC and Chicago. The bar front was a combination of mahogany and redwood burl, and the walls were mahogany veneer. A full mirror behind the bar gave the

effect of a fully circular bar.

The dining car was not only an epicurian delight, but a visual wonderland. The carpet, shades and drapes were burgundy, the leather upholstery on the chairs light blue, and on the sofas, yellow. The upper walls and ceiling were painted gold, while the bulkheads between the various dining and tavern sections were covered in either Flexwood or mirror squares.

Like the *Century*, the new *Broadway* was an all-roomette or all-bedroom train—section sleepers were history. In general the *Broadway* carried a baggage-mail car, bar-lounge car, three sleepers, sleeper-lounge, diner and the sleeper-observation.

That observation was perhaps the pinnacle of Loewy's artful design. The front lounge had leather upholstered settees at each window side, while the curved corner walls were covered with

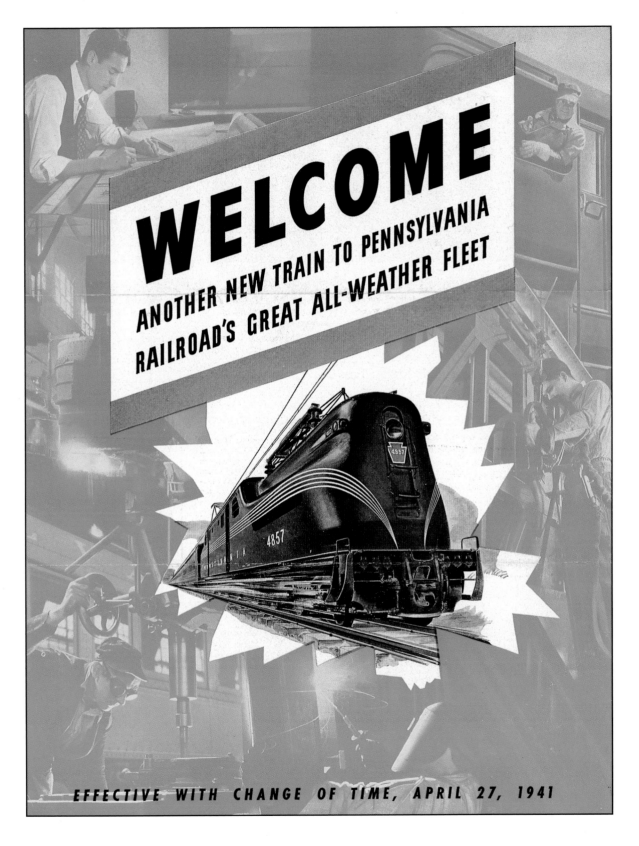

WELCOME

ANOTHER NEW TRAIN TO PENNSYLVANIA RAILROAD'S GREAT ALL-WEATHER FLEET

4857

EFFECTIVE WITH CHANGE OF TIME, APRIL 27, 1941

Pennsylvania's Jeffersonian was described by the railroad as the first deluxe all-coach train between New York and St. Louis at coach fares. The train ran on a 20 ½ hour schedule, making connections at St. Louis for Dallas, Fort Worth, Houston, Kansas City, Little Rock and Denver. Highlights of the train included radio in the observation-buffet-lounge car, complete dinners for as low as 75¢ and attendants in the cars.

Pennsylvania's all-weather fleet featured this giant duplex streamlined steam locomotive, a 6-4-4-6. Pennsy's locomotives of the 1940s were graceful-looking machines, and the road spared little expense to equip them with the latest mechanical advantages such as Timken roller bearings, feedwater heaters and boosters on trailing trucks.

Serving the Nation

On the Job 365 Days a Year !

Relax in luxury! This smart Pullman Lounge Car is furnished with divans, handsome easy chairs, "conversation corners"...radio...murals...mirrors...a beautiful beverage bar within easy hail—many appointments!

"Apartment for two!" Yes, this modern Compartment is all that. Arranged to provide spaciousness, it is completely self-contained, even to toilet facilities. Reserve one!

What do you see here? Yes, one of the great modern trains of Pennsylvania Railroad's fast All-Weather Fleet sweeping along in a dying sunset. But drench this scene with driving rain, sleet, snow—and that train would still be there, speeding onward!

For this great All-Weather Fleet is true to its name. Goes every day... gets you "there" every day...365 days a year.

Gets you there *in luxury*, too! In modern air-conditioned Pullmans with every appointment — or in Luxury Coaches with restful reclining seats. To many points you can enjoy the newest in Pullman private rooms — Roomettes, Duplex Rooms, Bedrooms, Compartments,

Drawing Rooms, Master Rooms as well as Section Sleepers. And however you go, Pullman or Coach, the cost is little — because FARES ARE LOW!

So, when you travel, select one of the trains of Pennsylvania Railroad's vast All-Weather Fleet. That's the best way to go anywhere, summer, winter — anytime!

★ ★ ★ ★
READY TO GO!
NEW YORK-CHICAGO . . . . . . 17 trains daily
Including *Broadway Limited, The General, The Admiral, The Pennsylvanian*
NEW YORK-ST. LOUIS . . . . . . 8 trains daily
WASHINGTON-ST. LOUIS . . . . . 8 trains daily
Led by *"Spirit of St. Louis"*
WASHINGTON-CHICAGO . . . . . 10 trains daily
Led by *Liberty Limited*
NEW YORK-WASHINGTON . . . 40 trains daily
Led by *The Congressional*
Plus a fleet of trains, daily, serving Philadelphia, Baltimore, Pittsburgh, Columbus, Cincinnati, Akron, Cleveland, Detroit, Dayton, Indianapolis, Louisville and other important cities.

VISIT WASHINGTON AT NO EXTRA COST! Between New York or Philadelphia *and many Western cities*, you can go or return via Washington on the Pennsylvania Railroad at NO EXTRA COST. Take advantage of liberal stop-over privileges.

Enjoy the "Extras" on these All-Coach Trains!

THE TRAIL BLAZER
17 hours — NEW YORK-CHICAGO
THE JEFFERSONIAN
20¼ hours — NEW YORK-ST. LOUIS

AT REGULAR LOW COACH FARES enjoy Observation-Buffet-Lounge Car ...Radio...Low-priced Meals (Dinner 75c; luncheon 65c; breakfast 50c)... Reserved individual reclining Seats... Attendants—many features.

Both trains provide through service to and from Washington also

THE SHORTEST ROUTE BETWEEN EAST AND WEST
Serves America's largest cities. Through car service to New England and the South. Convenient connections to all the West.

Pennsylvania Railroad
SAFETY   SPEED   COMFORT   COURTESY

154

Dick Bowers

The streamlined Broadway Limited *of the Pennsylvania Railroad operated on a 16-hour Chicago to New York schedule. Between Harrisburg and New York—195 miles—The Broadway was pulled by a streamlined electric locomotive. The passenger train had close-fitting vestibules, the absence of outside projections and inward curving "skirts" below the floor level concealing the electrical and air-conditioning mechanism. The train, painted in a rich tuscan red, was trimmed in flowing gold striping and lettering. The cars were assembled by welding to form continuous steel tubes, with the roofs and sides presenting perfectly flat outside surfaces.*

Part of the cover of the Pennsylvania Railroad timetable showing the giant duplex streamlined locomotives.

aluminum squares. The upper walls were finished in a metallic fabric, while the carpet was a green and tan weave. The rear observation section provided colored leather seating and cork covered walls. The two master bedrooms contained showers for the *creme-de-la-creme*.

Only the *Broadway* was totally re-equipped in 1938. However, the Fleet of Modernism included the *General* in New York-Chicago service, the *Spirit of St. Louis* between New York and St. Louis, and the *Liberty Limited* in Chicago-Wash-

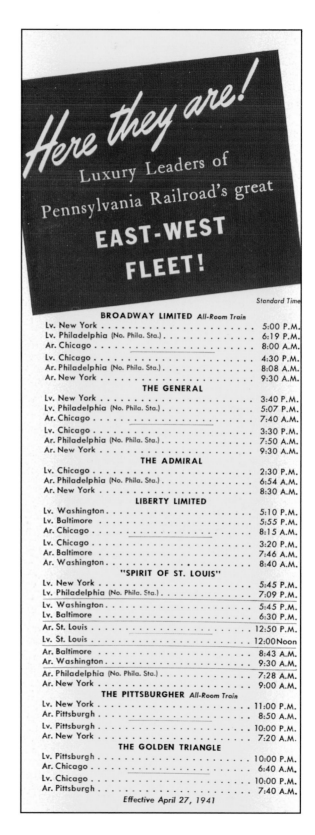

Here they are!

Luxury Leaders of
Pennsylvania Railroad's great

**EAST-WEST
FLEET!**

Standard Time

BROADWAY LIMITED All-Room Train

Lv. New York	5:00 P.M.
Lv. Philadelphia (No. Phila. Sta.)	6:19 P.M.
Ar. Chicago	8:00 A.M.
Lv. Chicago	4:30 P.M.
Ar. Philadelphia (No. Phila. Sta.)	8:08 A.M.
Ar. New York	9:30 A.M.

THE GENERAL

Lv. New York	3:40 P.M.
Lv. Philadelphia (No. Phila. Sta.)	5:07 P.M.
Ar. Chicago	7:40 A.M.
Lv. Chicago	3:30 P.M.
Ar. Philadelphia (No. Phila. Sta.)	7:50 A.M.
Ar. New York	9:30 A.M.

THE ADMIRAL

Lv. Chicago	2:30 P.M.
Ar. Philadelphia (No. Phila. Sta.)	6:54 A.M.
Ar. New York	8:30 A.M.

LIBERTY LIMITED

Lv. Washington	5:10 P.M.
Lv. Baltimore	5:55 P.M.
Ar. Chicago	8:15 A.M.
Lv. Chicago	3:20 P.M.
Ar. Baltimore	7:46 A.M.
Ar. Washington	8:40 A.M.

"SPIRIT OF ST. LOUIS"

Lv. New York	5:45 P.M.
Lv. Philadelphia (No. Phila. Sta.)	7:09 P.M.
Lv. Washington	5:45 P.M.
Lv. Baltimore	6:30 P.M.
Ar. St. Louis	12:50 P.M.
Lv. St. Louis	12:00 Noon
Ar. Baltimore	8:43 A.M.
Ar. Washington	9:30 A.M.
Ar. Philadelphia (No. Phila. Sta.)	7:28 A.M.
Ar. New York	9:00 A.M.

THE PITTSBURGHER All-Room Train

Lv. New York	11:00 P.M.
Ar. Pittsburgh	8:50 A.M.
Lv. Pittsburgh	10:00 P.M.
Ar. New York	7:20 A.M.

THE GOLDEN TRIANGLE

Lv. Pittsburgh	10:00 P.M.
Ar. Chicago	6:40 A.M.
Lv. Chicago	10:00 P.M.
Ar. Pittsburgh	7:40 A.M.

Effective April 27, 1941

Room to Relax ... Room to Roam
IN THESE NEW COACHES!

The thing you have always wanted in coach travel . . . *roominess!* Accomplished by Pennsylvania Railroad by installing *only 44 seats to the car.* More room to lean back . . . more room to stretch out. Fact is, more of *everything* for your enjoyment. Bigger panoramic windows . . . deeper luggage racks, with a compartment at the end for bulkier things . . .

brilliant fluorescent lighting—yet easy on the eyes . . . electro-pneumatic doors that open at finger's touch . . . air-conditioning . . . and, above all, a ride . . . easy, quiet and smooth. Step aboard one of the fine Pennsylvania Railroad trains equipped with these new overnight coaches and enjoy thorough comfort every mile of the way!

PENNSYLVANIA RAILROAD
Serving the Nation

Enjoy these Overnight Coaches on

THE TRAIL BLAZER
All-coach streamliner
NEW YORK-CHICAGO

THE JEFFERSONIAN
All-coach streamliner
NEW YORK-WASHINGTON-
ST. LOUIS

LIBERTY LIMITED
Premier train
WASHINGTON-BALTIMORE-
CHICAGO

at Low Coach Fares

EXTRA LARGE WASHROOMS

EASY-OPENING DOORS

"*Only 44 seats to the car,*" reads the ad promoting the new Pennsylvania passenger cars. The cars featured bigger windows, extra large washrooms and deeper luggage racks.

ington service. All received some new equipment including observation and dining cars and several all-room Pullmans. This massive fleet could handle any overflow from the *Broadway Limited*, making extra sections only rarely necessary. Like our service men and women, they did their job tirelessly throughout WWII.

SOUTHBOUND, FROM *SOUTH WIND* TO *SILVER METEOR*

Nothing brings the allure of tropical breezes and sandy beaches to mind more strongly than 12 inches or so of wind-driven Midwestern or Northeastern snow. As the Depression lessened, what better place to shake off such winter blues than Florida, via one of those fancy, new streamliners. Of course, the all-Pullman *Orange Blossom Special* was great for the "upper crust," but Mr. and Mrs. Joe Average could do just fine in a comfortable reclining seat-equipped streamliner.

Starting the parade was none other than the PRR, in full cooperation with equipment owner Seaboard Air Line. On February 2, 1939 at the Long Island station near the grounds of the 1939-40 World's Fair in New York City, the first *Silver Meteor* was christened, and proceeded to pick up its first passengers in Penn Station behind a GG-1 electric.

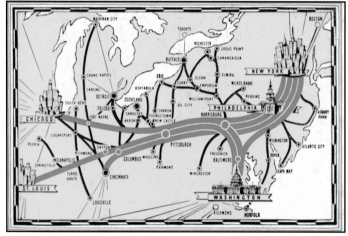

The Orange Blossom Special Going Through Orange Groves in Florida

There were many trains from the cold, snowy north to sunny Florida. In this view, the Orange Blossom Special makes its way past the many orange groves associated with Florida's economy.

The luxurious Orange Blossom Special was first introduced in 1925 and before World War II, operated in separate East Coast and West Coast sections. The Seaboard Air Line was the originator of the train.

G607 SUNNY FLORIDA
AS SEEN BY "STREAMLINER"

Diesel #3000 was one of 14 E-4A's built by EMC in 1938-1939. Here it's being assembled in the EMC shop.

The 7-car Budd-built streamliner contained the interior amenities expected of new streamliners such as air conditioning, reclining seat coaches, diner, lounge-observation and even an attractive stewardess/nurse. Combining that with speed—

about 24 hours New York City to Miami or St. Petersburg—and reliability, paid off. In four months the *Meteor* handled nearly 180,000 coach passengers. Even ticket scalpers were peddling bootleg *Meteor* tickets.

Seaboard's newly-acquired diesels in the late 1930s required some special publicity handling so they were lined up on parallel tracks for this photograph.

On the previous page, Seaboard's #3000 was seen new, but here it is being scrapped, returned again to EMD where it was constructed.

And no wonder, the train consisted of a baggage-dormitory-coach, three 60-seat coaches, a 30-seat coach-tavern, a full 48-seat diner and a 48-seat coach-lounge-observation. PRR GG-1's handled the train from New York to Washington, where Richmond, Fredericksburg & Potomac 4-8-4 steamers took over until Richmond, Virginia. There, new Seaboard Air Line EMD E-4 passenger diesels in citrus green, orange and yellow hauled

passengers south in grand and speedy style.

Competitors Atlantic Coast Line and Florida East Coast responded to the *Meteor's* arrival with their own order to Budd. On December 1, 1939 three 7-car *Champion* sets were placed in daily service between New York and Miami. Just like the *Meteor*, the Champions were handled by the PRR/RF&P duo between New York and Richmond.

EMD

Atlantic Coast Line's #501 was a 2,000-hp E unit, built between 1939-1941 by EMC.

Nearly identical to the SAL *Meteor* equipment, each set consisted of a dormitory-baggage-coach, three 60-seat coaches, a 54-seater with stewardess room, a 48-seat diner and tavern-lounge-observation. Like all Southern trains, one or two coaches were reserved for colored travelers.

Publicity-conscious FEC greeted the first southbound *Champion* in grand style. Waiting at the Jacksonville, Florida depot was its own Jacksonville-Miami streamliner, the *Henry M. Flagler*. Delivered within weeks of the *Champion*, and virtually identical in consist, the *Flagler* proceeded to pace the *Champion* side by side down the FEC double track main all the way to Miami—346 miles!

Hot on the heels of the *Champion*, Budd rolled out two more equipment sets for the *Meteor*, so on December 23, 1939 it, too, was a daily service

to Miami, and every third day to St. Petersburg.

In the Chicago market, an extraordinary cooperative effort by several railroads brought Florida streamliner service to the Windy City. Three individual train sets, each operating every third day over three competing lines, gave the customer all the service and variety needed.

On December 17, 1940 the *Dixie Flagler* went into this service, departing Chicago for Miami via Chicago & Eastern Illinois; the Louisville & Nashville; Nashville, Chattanooga & St. Louis; Atlantic Coast Line and Florida East Coast. In reality, this train was the 1939 FEC *Henry M. Flagler*, and for at least the first season, its red and yellow diesel locomotive so stated. Soon, the C&EI portion of the run was handled by a spiffy specially streamlined 4-6-2 Pacific.

The following day, the Illinois Central, Central

The Florida East Coast fielded a brightly-colored fleet of passenger diesels painted in red, yellow and silver. While the FEC didn't run through any particularly outstanding scenery, it did run the length of Florida, and its passenger trains hauled thousands of tourists to enjoy the warm weather and the ocean.

F. E. C. Streamliner
"The Champion"
at Miami, Florida

Budd

The Dixie Flagler was the successor to the Henry M. Flagler. It ran between Chicago and Miami; the Dixie Flagler alternated service with the City of Miami and the South Wind.

The smallish Chicago & Eastern Illinois Railroad, which ran from Chicago to St. Louis and Evansville, even streamlined its Dixie Flagler *steam locomotives to match the passenger cars.*

of Georgia, Atlantic Coast Line and Florida East Coast routing took effect with the vivid IC *City of Miami*. The Electro-Motive E-6 was citrus orange with a green bow wave rising from its sloping nose and cresting at its cab side windows. A scarlet pinstripe separated the bold colors. This finery stretched back over the entire train.

The only Pullman-Standard-built equipment in the Florida pool, it matched the other Budd consists of baggage-dormitory-coach, four reclining seat coaches, full diner and a dinette-observation. A Chicago-Miami one-way ticket was but $23.50, with a roundtrip reduction allowed. A full breakfast was $.50 and lunch or dinner just $.60.

Finally, on December 19, 1940 the Pennsy,

Louisville & Nashville, Atlantic Coast Line and Florida East Coast routing took place. This was another 7-car Budd consist, but painted PRR tuscan red, and handled—on the PRR and L&N portions—by streamlined 4-6-2 Pacific steam locomotives. Smartly styled maroon uniformed attendants and a keystone silhouetted *South Wind* emblem left no doubt as to who supplied this equipment set.

All sets over all routes were jammed as the 1941 season became the season of world war. The *Champion* and *Silver Meteor* both received Pullman cars for the winter 1941-42 season, while the other three services had to wait until the postwar period.

Another Great Streamliner for The Illinois Central

CITY OF MIAMI

BUILT BY PULLMAN-STANDARD

THE WORLD'S LARGEST BUILDERS OF RAILROAD AND TRANSIT EQUIPMENT

AMONG the millions of Americans who have grown so tired of waiting for Spring that they've decided to go in search of Summer are certain lucky thousands who will make that joyful journey in swift magnificence—from Chicago to Miami in only 29½ hours—on the streamliner—*City of Miami*—which Pullman-Standard recently completed for the Illinois Central System.

Pullman-Standard streamliners now link America's greatest cities

As still another Illinois Central streamliner, its advent marks one more important step in that trend which is making trains of this modern type available in every section of the country.

Who has been responsible for this trend . . . one of the grandest marches in the history of transportation? We, of this generation, who have watched it come into being and mature within a period of six years, know!

Pullman-Standard started it by building the first lightweight train . . . by establishing the standards of strength and safety by which all other construction is measured . . . and by building over 72%* of the streamlined units purchased by the railroads and The Pullman Company.

Pioneering railroads made it possible by investing the millions of dollars needed to transform blueprints into realities.

But even more important, the real life and impulse to this movement came from you, the American traveling public. For it has been your enthusiastic reception of Pullman-Standard-built streamliners which has made them the most popular and profitable group of trains in the country and is justifying the railroads in ordering them in ever-increasing numbers!

*When this advertisement was written

> Luxury Coach Diesel Streamliner "City of Miami"
> Lv. Chicago 9:40 A.M. Ar. Miami next day 4:10 P.M.
> Lv. Miami 6:25 P.M. Ar. Chicago next day 10:55 P.M.
> *(Departures every third day)*
> For further information regarding this service, write Illinois Central System, 501 Central Station, Chicago, Ill.

PULLMAN-STANDARD CAR MANUFACTURING COMPANY—CHICAGO

In addition to railroad passenger cars, Pullman-Standard designs and manufactures freight, subway, elevated and street cars, trackless trolleys, air-conditioning systems, chilled tread car wheels and a complete line of car repair parts.
Copyright 1941, by Pullman-Standard Car Manufacturing Company

1) **The Coaches,** colorfully decorated with Floridian scenes, provide such special comforts as individual reading lights, a car reserved for women and children, and Stewardess-Registered Nurse service.

2) **Bamboo Grove,** the beautiful tavern-lounge-observation car, has oversized windows to admit floods of sunlight and scenery; its comfortable easy-chairs are movable so they can be drawn up to the writing desk or radio or turned for conversation.

3) **The Bar,** with its bamboo decorations and huge pictorial murals, calls to mind the amusing cafés of the tropic lands and is completely air-conditioned, as are all cars on this sumptuous train.

4) **Palm Garden,** the diner—crowning touch for many of those who go to Florida the streamlined way—offers menus built around the exotic dishes and delicacies distinguishing that fruitful land.

"Tops" IN STREAMLINERS ARE BUILT BY *Pullman-Standard*

The City of Miami *began service on December 18, 1940 with a seven-car lightweight consist. Built by Pullman-Standard, the train made the Chicago to Miami run in 29 ½ hours. The colorful orange and green train left Chicago at 9:40 a.m. and arrived in Miami at 4:10 p.m. the next day, after traveling over several different routes.*

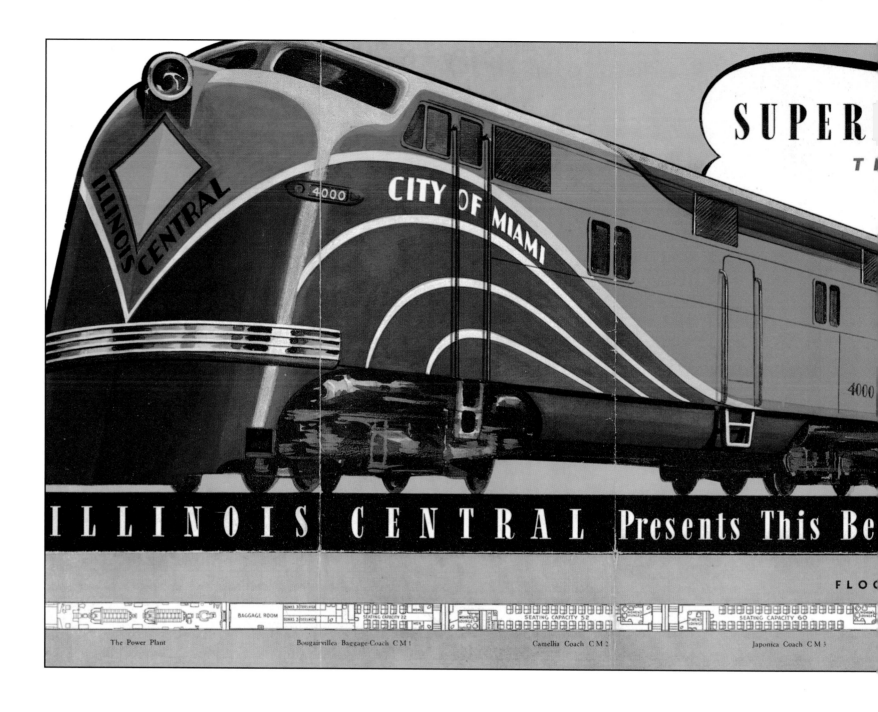

SUPER

T

ILLINOIS CENTRAL Presents This Be

FLOO

The Power Plant　　　　Bougairvillea Baggage-Coach C M 1　　　　Camellia Coach C M 2　　　　Japonica Coach C M 3

SOUTHERN 'SERVES THE SOUTH,'
STREAMLINER STYLE

The Southern Railway was aware of the Florida streamliner success since their 1939 introduction. As the premier road between the Eastern seaboard and the major cities of the old South, the Southern was not about to be left off the bandwagon. Atlanta, Birmingham, Chattanooga, and of course New Orleans would soon have Southern streamliner service.

In mid-1940, the Southern placed orders with Pullman-Standard for streamlined coaches, lounges, tavern-observations, and with Alco and Electro-Motive for the diesel power to pull them. Responding to the economic realities of the day, the *Southerner* was a coach-only service. The

IN BEAUTY... SUPREME IN COMFORT

LUXURY COACH DIESEL STREAMLINER

City of Miami

CHICAGO - MIAMI

ILLINOIS CENTRAL

...tiful Train Serving America's Loveliest Playgrounds

PLAN

Palm Garden—Diner   Hibiscus Coach C M 4   Poinsettia Coach C M 5   Bamboo Grove Tavern-Lounge-Observation

Tennessean likewise was to be coach-only, but actually carried one or more heavyweight Pullmans from the beginning.

On March 31, 1941 the inaugural *Southerner* left New York's Penn Station behind a PRR GG-1 and sped south. Equipped with reclining seats, air conditioning, indirect lighting and coordinated pastel color scheme, it made the omission of Pullman space seem incidental. At Washington D.C., motive power became a brand new green and white Electro-Motive E-6 diesel, and the streamliner took to home rails for Atlanta, Birmingham and New Orleans. Only 30 hours separated the cold of New York from the Mardi Gras potential and Cajun cooking of New Orleans. The tavern-observation did its part providing immediate winter relief.

Shortly thereafter, on May 17, 1941 a sister service, the *Tennessean* joined the fleet. This train gave streamliner service to patrons between Memphis and Washington DC, via Bristol and Chattanooga, Tennessee. Similarly equipped, its tavern-observation likewise was extremely popular. The 25 hours between Memphis and Washington passed quickly, and plenty of connections with New York and beyond were available.

The *Tennessean* passed from Southern trackage to that of the Norfolk & Western between Bristol, Tennessee and Lynchburg, Virginia. On the N&W portion, by 1943 the train was headed by one of 11 company-built 4-8-4's of majestic proportions and design. Capable of rolling 80 mph and putting out over 5000 hp, in 1950 three more of these streamlined goliaths were the last streamlined passenger steam power built in America. They fended off diesel conquest until 1959.

On Southern rails southwest of Bristol, the *Tennessean* was frequently powered by a chisel-nosed Alco DL-109 passenger locomotive. The descent of WWII and technological shortcomings made the DL-109 a rare beast. Coupled to the silvery streamliner, it turned many a head in the rural Appalachian countryside the train traversed daily. It was not only on the Southern that heads turned to admire a new, flashy streamliner.

SOUTHERN BELLE: STREAMLINED HOSPITALITY

The joint operation of the Kansas City Southern and the Louisiana & Arkansas in 1939 set the stage for another new Southern streamliner. Kansas City and New Orleans were about to be connected in a new way.

On September 1, 1940 service between the two cities started. The 4-car *Belle* was pulled by EMC's first E-3—the former demonstrator—or a twin sister, and was color-coordinated from front coupler shroud to observation. Resplendent in a dark— almost black—green with yellow and red highlight stripes, those in the vicinity took note of the *Belle's* passage.

Although a road of modest means, KCS poured into the *Belle* all the latest features. When Pullman-Standard was finished, the new equipment included seats with foot rests, air conditioning, Pullmans, diner, and that mark of excellence, the tavern-observation car. Of course the coaches were segregated, but that was just the way it was.

Instantly popular, the *Belle* was a colorful addition to a world about to plunge into war. Not only would the *Belle* survive WWII, but re-equipped, the snappy streamliner lasted until nearly 1970.

In the South, all the pre-war coach streamliners were now in operation, but not quite so for the extra-fare Pullman service. Their final example was to brighten an otherwise grim spring of 1942 on the Main Line of Mid-America.

ILLINOIS CENTRAL'S FINEST

Deep in the depressing war news of late April, 1942 came an unexpected announcement from the Illinois Central. Finally, after wrangling with the War Production Board, and cajoling builders Pullman and Electro-Motive Division (GM), its long anticipated *Panama Limited* was to be placed in service on May 1, 1942.

Delivered in IC's new chocolate brown and orange with yellow striping livery, twin Electro-Motive E-6 diesels headed up the 12-car speedster as it awaited departure from New Orleans toward Chicago or St. Louis. Each A unit carried *Panama Limited* in script on its flank. Since it was wartime, no fancy gala marked this last pre-war-designed-streamliner inaugural, but still the consist was noteworthy.

Behind the locomotives was a baggage-dormitory which even carried the train name across the IC diamond emblem. Six sleepers of section, roomette and bedroom configuration followed, then the sleeper-lounge and full diner. An 18-roomette car was next, then a bedroom-compartment-drawing room car followed, and the sleeper-observation completed the train.

Of particular note was the Vieux Carre section of New Orleans French Quarter styling in the lounge. Containing six seats out of the lounge total of 14, the Vieux Carre's wrought ironwork, potted ivy and inlaid wood bar made it a centerpiece. Its dining section seated 32, with photos of the antebellum South on the bulkheads. Quality of both food and service became legendary. An unusual feature of the Panama was a complimentary full dinner—presuming you had paid the $4 extra service charge. Most patrons had, and con-

THE TENNESSEAN

Southern's Washington to Memphis Tennessean *train ran through Lynchburg, Bristol, Knoxville and Chattanooga. Through sleeping cars were assigned between New York and Memphis.*

sidered the dinner itself well worth the money. Some claimed dining on the *Panama* was a worthy introduction to breakfast at Brennan's, or dinner at Antoine's in New Orleans.

The *Panama* was the last prewar streamlined all-Pullman train to be introduced in North America. This fact places it in the rarified company of the *Super Chief, 20th Century, Broadway Limit-*

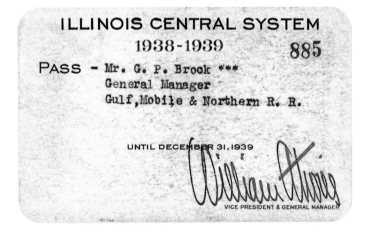

SOUTHERN
RAILWAY SYSTEM

1939   No. B 8183

PASS   A. E. Herring--
        A.G.P.A., C&G Ry.,
        Columbus, Miss.

BETWEEN ALL STATIONS UNTIL DECEMBER 31, 1939
UNLESS OTHERWISE ORDERED OR RESTRICTED BELOW AND SUBJECT TO CONDITIONS ON BACK

VALID WHEN COUNTERSIGNED BY P. B. PARKE OR W. P. KNOTT

NOT GOOD ON TRAINS 37 AND 38

                                    VICE PRESIDENT

ILLINOIS CENTRAL SYSTEM
1938-1939   885

PASS - Mr. G. P. Brock ***
       General Manager
       Gulf, Mobile & Northern R. R.

UNTIL DECEMBER 31, 1939

                        VICE PRESIDENT & GENERAL MANAGER

Southern's classy Southerner *started service in March of 1941, leaving New York's Penn Station behind a GG-1 electric headed for New Orleans. While it was a coach-only service, it featured reclining seats, indirect lighting and an interior pastel color scheme.*

ed and a handful of others. Its 18-hour overnight schedule through perhaps the greatest density of military installations in the country, filled both its public and private rooms with military contractors and officers of all service branches.

If the *Panama Limited* did not exude fun and frivolity, it certainly rose to meet its patriotic wartime duty. Night after night the *Panama* carried its business and military personages on their way between its terminal cities. No more could

Southern Railway System Proudly Announces

THE SOUTHERNER
THE TENNESSEAN

BUILT BY PULLMAN-STANDARD
THE WORLD'S LARGEST BUILDERS OF RAILROAD AND TRANSIT EQUIPMENT

THE OBSERVATION-TAVERN CAR—beautifully appointed in every detail—provides hostess as well as porter service. Its full facilities are always available to everyone traveling on these new single-fare streamliners.

*"The Southerner" begins operating between New York and New Orleans—via Atlanta and Birmingham—on or about March 15. "The Tennessean" will be placed in service between Washington and Memphis on or about April 15.

Mark how rapid has been the increase in points between which streamlined rail service is available. For example, their number is being swelled by the Southern Railway's purchase of these new trains to operate between New York and New Orleans and Memphis and Washington.*

No stronger—safer trains have ever been built

Mark, too, how frequently Pullman-Standard is the builder. The reason is the soundest in the world—*safety!* For, as the creator of streamlining in America, Pullman-Standard co-operated with the railroads and the government in establishing the standards of strength and safety to which all modern passenger cars should be built, regardless of the materials employed.

Railroad men know that—and recognizing that there are no stronger, safer trains than those constructed by Pullman-Standard, have

THE COACHES are ultra-modern, streamlined, air-conditioned, and equipped with sofa-soft seats, adjustable for relaxation; glare-free illumination, extra wide full-vision windows, up-to-date washrooms.

turned to this company for 70%† of the new equipment which has been purchased.

You have made Pullman-Standard Streamliners Gross the Highest Revenues

If a second reason is needed, you have supplied that, too. For the preference you show for the smoother, easier riding streamliners this company builds is unmistakable. By filling them to capacity as fast as they have gone into service, you have made them top all other fleets of trains in earnings and in popularity!

†When this advertisement was written

PULLMAN-STANDARD CAR MANUFACTURING COMPANY—CHICAGO

Copyright 1941, by Pullman-Standard Car Manufacturing Company

"Tops" IN STREAMLINERS ARE BUILT BY *Pullman-Standard*

In fall of 1940 the Southern Belle *came on the streamliner scene, sponsored by the Kansas City Southern. The train was pulled by EMC's original demonstrator E-3A or its sister unit.*

The Observation Lounge is one of the sparkling departures which has gained for this train, the *Southern Belle*, the reputation of "providing all the extras at no extra fare." For its privileges, including radio, magazine racks, and game facilities, are available to all passengers without additional charge.

The Cafe Lounge is spacious. Its tables well separated . . . its walls, ceilings and floor completely insulated so that neither crowding nor noise nor hurried service spoil your enjoyment of truly delicious food.

The Skyline Bar decorated in huge murals and luxurious modern appointments provides a cosmopolitan background against which to encounter old friends or enjoy encounters with new acquaintances.

The Chair Car, like all other units on this modern train, is completely air-conditioned and, in it, the comfort of passengers is deftly administered by registered stewardess nurses as well as trained *Southern Belle* porters.

In addition to railroad passenger cars, Pullman-Standard designs and manufactures freight, subway, elevated and street cars, trackless trolleys, air-conditioning systems, chilled tread car wheels and a complete line of car repair parts. A large percentage of this company's productive capacity is also engaged in the manufacture of defense material.

Another Illustrious Streamliner—
SOUTHERN BELLE

OWNED AND OPERATED BY KANSAS CITY SOUTHERN—LOUISIANA & ARKANSAS LINES

BUILT BY PULLMAN-STANDARD

THE WORLD'S LARGEST BUILDERS OF RAILROAD AND TRANSIT EQUIPMENT

In purchasing this magnificent new streamliner, *Southern Belle*, for service between Kansas City and New Orleans, the Kansas City Southern—Louisiana & Arkansas Lines acted on the sound principle that no consideration should outweigh safety . . . so they specified Pullman-Standard Construction.

There are no safer trains than Pullman-Standard's

Out of Pullman-Standard's 82 year experience . . . out of research before it gave streamlining to America . . . out of its constant constructive work with the physical properties of all available fabricating materials . . . and out of the privilege it has had for more than twenty-five years of collaborating periodically with the government and the railroads in establishing the specifications for strength and safety to which all railroad equipment should be built, have come the Pullman-Standard trains whose strength and safety are exceeded by no others now in service.

Your enthusiastic patronage has made streamliners possible and profitable

As a result of their safety, no less than beauty and luxury, Pullman-Standard's streamliners have established the two other most envied records in railroading: 1) the most popular trains in operation; 2) the most profitable trains. But in the last analysis these have been your achievement. You, the public, have made them possible through demonstrating your overwhelming preference for Pullman-Standard streamliners by filling them to capacity as fast as they have gone into service! And the railroads have answered by buying 70%* of the new equipment they have purchased from Pullman-Standard.

PULLMAN-STANDARD CAR MANUFACTURING COMPANY—CHICAGO

Copyright 1941, by Pullman-Standard Car Manufacturing Company

*When this advertisement was written

"Tops" IN STREAMLINERS ARE BUILT BY Pullman-Standard

be asked, and the good times would have to wait out the war.

With the *Panama Limited*, the pre-war Streamliner Era ended, when so much design talent and new materials went into the birth of each new train. If the streamliner of the 30s was special, its postwar offspring was more democratic. The all-Pullman cachet was replaced by the dome and Slumbercoach.

It is rather ironic that the IC's first streamliner, the unadorned *Green Diamond* ended the articulated motor train chapter of the Streamliner Era, while its luxurious *Panama Limited* closed out the prewar chapter. However, the patrons of the Main Line of Mid-America had stellar pleasures awaiting them at war's end.

Originally begun in 1928, the Kansas City Southern's Flying Crow *carries an early E unit diesel on its trip between Kansas City and Port Arthur, Texas.*

The American Streamliner, Postwar Years, *which will conclude the Streamliner story, is now in the development stage.*

173

Private Railroad Cars

Private railroad passenger cars still roam the rails. Below is a listing of a few of them. Additional information can be obtained about private cars by writing the American Association of Private Railroad Car Owners, Inc., c/o M. Diane Elliot, 106 N. Carolina Ave., S.E., Washington, D.C. 20003.

For information on *Private Varnish*, a magazine devoted to private railroad passenger cars, write AAPRCO, Inc., P.O. Box 50221, Pasadena, CA 91115-0221.

Babbling Brook

CAR NAME:

Babbling Brook was built by Budd in 1949 for the New York Central's *New England States* train between Boston and Chicago. Focal point of the stainless steel car is the observation lounge, but the car also includes a dining area, kitchen and four bedrooms. Frank Dowd, Jr., P.O. Box 35430, Charlotte, N.C. 28235

Colonial Crafts entered service on the Pennsylvania Railroad at Chicago in June of 1949. The 85-foot car offers three bed-

Colonial Crafts

rooms, drawing room, a buffet and a large lounge. Rod Fishburn, 9303 Crystal View Drive, Tujunga, CA 91042-3049

Pacific Grove was built by Budd in 1940 for the Seaboard as a blunt end observation car with buffet, 24-seat lounge, 30 coach seats and a stewardess' room. The

Pacific Grove

car ran on the *Silver Meteor*. Richard Losch, 21050 Upper Zayante Rd., Los Gatos, CA 95030

Glacier Park was built by Pullman in 1948 as a lightweight sleeper and features 20 beds—13 lowers and 7 uppers in 4 single bedrooms, 5 twin bedrooms and 2 triple bedrooms. The car has served on the FEC and the CN. Bob Stevens, Jr., P.O. Box 5027, Helena, MT 59604

Imperial Sands was built by Pullman in 1942 and operated on railroads such as the Union Pacific, Southern Pacific and C&NW. The ten bedrooms in the 85-foot

Imperial Sands

car can sleep 22. Donald Smith, 21 Patriot's Rd., Morris Plains, NJ 07950

Northern Sky is a blunt end dome car featuring four double staterooms with a sleeping capacity of 8. Rooms include a

Northern Sky

lounge, upper level dome, kitchen and staterooms. A complete home theater entertainment system is located throughout the car. Louis Nowicki, 2816 W. Grange Ave., Milwaukee, WI 53221

Palm Beach was built as Seaboard Air Line Railroad car #15 in 1949 and ran on the *Silver Meteor*. The car features a

Palm Beach

lounge seating 16, or will accommodate 8 for dinner. There is also a buffet and five double bedrooms, a shower and other amenities. Robert E. Nelson, Box 10208, Green Bay, WI 54307-0208

Salisbury Beach is a Pullman-Standard stainless-sided sleeper built for the B&M

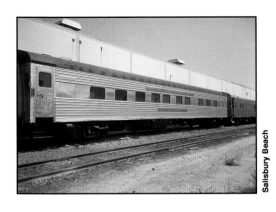

Salisbury Beach

Silver Slope

Vista Canyon is a square end observation lounge car built by Pullman in 1947 for the Santa Fe's *Super Chief*. The car sleeps 14: two in the bedroom and three in each drawing room. The lounge seats 12. Last service on the Santa Fe was about 1968. Fred and Dale Springer, P.O. Box 1163, Salado, TX 76571

Railroad in the mid-1950s. The car ran on the *State of Maine* and the *Montrealer* and features six roomettes, four bedrooms and six sections. Like other cars, it has undergone extensive refurbishing. Tom

Pearson, 10 Autumn Hill Lane, Laguna Hills, CA 92653-6016

Silver Slope was built by Budd in 1952 for the CB&O to run on the *California Zephyr*. It features 10 roomettes and 6 double bedrooms plus a porter's room. The car ran in Amtrak service until 1978. William Butterworth, 2509 Lakeway Dr., Shreveport, LA 71109

Vista Canyon

Index